PRAISE FOR
unbroken

"'When everyone is moving towards depravity, no one seems to be moving, but if someone stops, he shows up the others who are rushing on, by acting as a fixed point" – Blaise Pascal.'
In her book *Unbroken*, Katherine Hager, stops amidst a secular and swift current which is sweeping up families into a maelstrom of chaos and confusion. Then with Christ-centered and comprehensive clarity, leads readers to the 'fixed point' of God's Word, to the divine blueprint for motherhood. This isn't just another manual on child-rearing, it is a rescue of generations."

—MARGARET ASHMORE, AUTHOR OF
THE SUN ALWAYS RISES AND WOMEN'S CONFERENCE SPEAKER

"I love Katherine's approach to exhorting mamas: she walks through 2 Timothy, meditating on the unique way it speaks to mothering. More than a mommy pep-talk, this book is a powerful call to mothering with conviction and courage. You will be challenged to pray more fervently, to study God's Word more deeply, and to disciple more intentionally. I highly recommend it to moms in any season of life!"

—SARAH HANCOCK, FOUNDER OF
BRIGHT LIGHTS MINISTRIES, AUTHOR AND SPEAKER

unbroken

MOTHERING IN A WORLD
GONE WRONG

EQUIPPEDMaMa
2 TIMOTHY 3:16-17

KATHERINE
HAGER

unbroken

MOTHERING IN A WORLD
GONE WRONG

ISBN: 979-8-9986504-1-3 (Paperback)

ISBN: 978-1-7341581-9-9 (Hardcover)

ISBN: 979-8-9986504-0-6 (eBook)

Library of Congress Control Number: 2025904518

Editor: Kimberly Schumate

Book formatting and cover design: Becky's Graphic Design®, LLC
www.BeckysGraphicDesign.com

Printed in the United States of America

EQUIPPEDMAMA
2 TIMOTHY 3:16-17

For my children.

May you live faithfully in a world gone wrong.

CONTENTS

INTRODUCTION

"**MY WATER HAD JUST** broken. We needed to go to the hospital, and he was in the shower!" My friend recalled the harrowing story of how their daughter made her debut into the world.

"Seriously, he took a 45-minute shower. I was trying not to be that nasty wife, but come on! I was just standing downstairs all ready to go, trying to make it through the contractions when he finished. We finally made it to the hospital, and I was in active labor and rushed immediately to a delivery room."

"But then she didn't even come for several hours," interrupted her husband wryly. "I knew I had time."

We all laughed as our friends reminisced about the dramatic nature of their child's birth. Their story created a springboard for us to share about our third child's stressful birth. Our situations were not identical, but they related.

In our culture, relatability is everything. The very structure of our society is built around relatability. Often church fellowship groups are divided by demographics like age or marital status. Young couple's Bible study. Moms of little ones' study. Study for divorcees. These are often the ways we see groups created in order to give continuity of experience and a level of camaraderie.

Often the need for relatability also fuels the type of media we consume. While dating, women may read about relationship purity, or tips for emotional and sexual intimacy. Once married, women read studies on how to communicate more effectively, how to craft a warm home environment, and how to make their husband feel loved. Motherhood seems to be the pinnacle for Christian women's advice books. Replete with advice from potty training to prayer time with children, this genre of books promises to help any woman mother like a pro. Many hope to live better, to steward time more wisely, and to shepherd hearts more effectively. And many of these books are good and have definite value.

However, in our information-crazed culture, we have devalued the worth of absolute truth and elevated relatable information. At a time when our faith is attacked by our culture, Christian women seem less grounded in the Word than ever before. We seek to relate to God, rather than to know Him. We want to know Scripture to see how it fits in our situations and our lives. We seek to be ministered to by His Word rather than to understand the One who inspired these words.

While we live and work and raise our children, the world grows dark. Many women voice concern over the future of their children as they see moral lines drawn within our culture. Attacks are being made on the people of God and His standards for living. This is reason for concern no matter the age of your children. In this season, we don't need one more book on the subject—another mom telling us that she, too, is anxious about the state of the world. We won't benefit by fixating on how terrible things could be, or are, or might become.

We are wise to be prepared. We are wise to know and understand the heart of God and the power of His Word. We need to search His Word and understand how we can become more Christ-like.

This book wasn't written while lounging on a comfy couch, in a warm climate-controlled room, with a hot drink in one hand and the scented glow of a decorative candle glittering in the background. Well, okay, *this* book was, but the epistle was not.

This epistle was also *not* the product of one mom wanting to commiserate with another mom about postpartum hormones, breastfeeding struggles, or the challenges of disciplining a two-year-old while battling morning sickness. The epistle wasn't written by a mother at all, nor was the audience a biological child. It was written in a very concrete space in history, penned by one of the most influential men in the Christian faith.

The Apostle Paul was living in circumstances drastically different from ours. His story is a historical fact, not an anecdote or fictional narrative to entertain us. Through his divinely inspired letter written to his spiritual son, Timothy, mothers today can glean valuable lessons on mothering. We might not identify with Paul, but we can learn from him.

Like many generations before us, women fear the future and the present. We fear the world into which we bring our little ones. We fear what they might face and how they might respond to challenges. We fear if we are doing enough to prepare them. We want assurance that we are shielding them from danger, equipping them for a future, and establishing them for the best way forward.

Paul wrote 2 Timothy with similar motivation. He knew his time on earth was almost finished. As he anticipated his death, he penned this final letter to his dear friend and spiritual son—a young preacher with whom Paul had developed a close relationship. This letter was to be a final exhortation to follow Christ well, and to serve Him sacrificially. This was Paul's goodbye, which encompassed his desires for Timothy's stable future.

Paul's physical conditions at the writing of this letter would make anyone cringe. He was incarcerated as part of the Emperor Nero's persecution of Christians following the great Roman fire. In A.D. 64 a blaze broke out, destroying the majority of the city. As rumors circulated that the Emperor of Rome had ordered the torching, Nero sought a scapegoat on whom to pin the blame. The Christian people were a group already disliked by the general populace, and several of the unharmed districts were heavily populated by these believers. It was a perfect alibi. And so, the burning of Rome initiated a deluge of Christian persecution. Individuals were arrested and killed for their religious beliefs. Men, women, and children were burned alive, fed to wild animals, and victimized in countless and horrific ways. At that moment, their world was bleak.

Paul had been imprisoned in Rome shortly before the writing of his first epistle to Timothy. That detention had been with some level of dignity—being held in his home, he had enjoyed a few limited freedoms. This second imprisonment, approximately six years later, lacked any physical comforts.

Yet, replete through this letter we see the power of God driving this saint on. We find unshakable faith and divine peace. In its pages we are privy to the beautiful work of God's Spirit, conforming a man to Himself. We discover discipleship that means something and is profoundly life-changing. Most of all, we see something worth emulating.

We are exposed to a deeper understanding of God's sustaining grace and our own abject need for Him. We begin to grasp how able He is to keep our precious little ones safe, even in our absence.

Are you a mother of little ones? Perhaps with no children of your own, but a mentor to young women. Or maybe your children are grown and giving you grandchildren to shepherd. Whatever your maternal situation, this letter is for you.

As you read, don't look to find yourself in the text, but seek to learn the heart of God, and how He proved faithful to produce unshakable faith in the life of the Apostle Paul. Read with anticipation, Mama, and discover the unbreakable strength God has to offer you.

Guard, through the Holy Spirit who dwells in us,
the treasure which has been entrusted to you.

2 TIMOTHY 1:14

ONE

KNOW THE AUTHOR, KNOW THE AUDIENCE

Paul, an apostle of Christ Jesus by the will of God,
according to the promise of life in Christ Jesus,
To Timothy, my beloved son: Grace, mercy, and peace
from God the Father and Christ Jesus our Lord.

2 TIMOTHY 2:1-2

KISSING WAR GOODBYE IS perhaps one of the most iconic photos of World War II, featuring the embrace of a sailor and nurse in Times Square at the announcement of V-J Day. At first glance, it is a romantic reunion between war-torn lovers. Likely those who have purchased the famous print assume that the two were reunited after active duty, or perhaps had met and fell in love on some dangerous overseas placement, much like a Hollywood movie.

The reality, however, is less idyllic. On August 14, 1945, Greta Zimmer, a dental hygienist separated from her Austrian parents because of the war, heard news that the conflict had ended. Throughout the morning, patients came into the dentist's office buzzing with joy. Greta waited for an opportune moment to verify this news at the Times Square News zipper where major headlines were posted.

The same day, Petty Officer First Class George Mendonsa was enjoying the last few hours of leave, which he had spent with his new girlfriend, Rita Petry. He and Rita had gone to a movie in the city when the news of the war's end had interrupted the show. The couple rushed out to celebrate, and made their way to the subway station near Times Square.

Overwhelmed by the long-anticipated end of the nightmare, George saw Greta in her hygienist uniform, and believing she was a nurse—having served maimed soldiers overseas—he was drawn to her. Without so much as knowing her name, he grabbed Greta and kissed her, with his girlfriend only a short distance away. Then he and Rita continued their torrid path of celebration. This moment was captured by Alfred Eisenstaedt, a *Life* Magazine photographer, who immortalized this fleeting moment of reckless revelry.[1]

Context matters.

Misconceptions are often formed without adequate information, as illustrated by this photo of the kissing sailor. Relationships can go awry due to lack of understanding. Scripture can be misinterpreted out of lack of context. These are serious mistakes to make! It is always wise to dive into any passage of Scripture knowing the basic facts about the writer of the book and the audience for whom he wrote it. Honing our own discipline in order to understand the context of Scripture is paramount so that we can grasp its original meaning.

Know the Author

2 Timothy was Paul's farewell letter to his son in the faith, Timothy. The beginning of this epistle shares a brief intro-

duction of the author (and the audience). Inspired by the Holy Spirit and impressed by the brevity of his remaining time on earth, Paul words his message precisely and powerfully.

He begins with, *"Paul, an apostle of Christ Jesus by the will of God, according to the promise of life in Christ Jesus"* (2 Timothy 1:1). His succinct introduction was unmistakable to his readers, and also hope-infused. Although Timothy already knew Paul's testimony, he was reminded of this apostle's calling and position in Christ. This was the same Paul, once called Saul of Tarsus, who stood with the ruthless murders of Stephen, and was responsible for "ravaging the church, entering house after house, and dragging off men and women, he would put them in prison" (Acts 8:3). This was the man who had been chosen by Christ to be an ambassador for His Gospel and servant to His body, the church.

There was no other way to explain Paul's dramatic change other than the calling of Jesus Christ. Acts 9 chronicles how Paul had spearheaded a campaign against Christians, seeking jurisdiction from the high priest to incarcerate believers for their faith. It was in the very act of carrying out this wicked deed that Christ reproved him, struck him blind, and revealed Himself to him.

"I am Jesus whom you are persecuting" (Acts 9:5b). Then the Lord orchestrated the regaining of Paul's sight at the hand of a Christ-follower named Ananias. Hesitant to approach this man who had wreaked such havoc on the church, Ananias was offered encouragement.

"But the Lord said to him, 'Go, for he is a chosen instrument of Mine, to bear My name before the Gentiles and kings and the sons of Israel; for I will show him how much he must suffer for My name's sake" (Acts 9:15-16). With his vision restored, Paul quickly proved the veracity of the Lord's words. His actions confirmed that he was, indeed, chosen of the Lord, and as promised, he suffered greatly for his testimony of being a Christ-follower.

The next decades of Paul's life were filled with fruitful ministry and fierce mistreatment because of his affiliation with Jesus. To introduce himself as an apostle of Jesus Christ was more than a simple statement of fact. It was Paul's identity; his vocation; his condemnation, and his future.

Timothy already knew Paul's identity in Christ. Still, it was no accident that the condemned apostle, awaiting imminent execution in a fetid cell reminded his young friend of his testimony. He was not Paul, the man who had given up his life to serve Jesus. He was no poor criminal begging for release. The meaning for his life and impending death was entirely based in the *"promise of life in Christ Jesus."*

Paul had mentioned this promise of life in his previous letter, the epistle 1 Timothy, and had elaborated on it further in his letter to the church at Colossae when he wrote, "Set your mind on the things above, not on the things that are on earth. For you have died and your life is hidden with Christ in God. When Christ, who is our life, is revealed, then you also will be revealed with Him in glory" (Colossians 3:2-4).

Now Paul reiterated this constant hope that he had, even in the worst of circumstances. Jesus Christ was his life. Although he had no earthly reason to hope, he had every spiritual reason. Because of his faith in the Lord Jesus Christ, he had the expectation of the promise of eternal life after his earthly death.

Know the Audience

To Timothy, my beloved son: Grace, mercy, and peace
from God the Father and Christ Jesus our Lord.

2 TIMOTHY 1:2

Mamas know what it means to love. From the moment of a positive pregnancy test or adoption placement, a woman's heart is full with both excitement and fear. With the entrance of a tiny life, sacrifice begins. Breastfeeding mamas give up food groups to accommodate their infant's needs. Mamas of foster children give up their expectations of what their family should be like as they serve their temporary or forever treasures. Mamas of children with disabilities sacrifice their resources to give their child opportunity to excel. There is nothing a mama won't do for her child.

Paul's greeting echoes the same fervor of affection. He addresses the letter to Timothy "my beloved son." The original Greek adjective, agapētos, is the same used by God the Father to address Jesus at the time of His baptism.[2] It carries the meaning of being esteemed, dear, favored, and worthy of love.[3] Paul had written an epistle to Timothy before, and that time he had called the man "his true child in the faith."[4] The original word Paul used carried the meaning of being a legitimate son, which was reasonable, as Paul had been the man to lead Timothy to the Lord. This epistle is marked with an intensity of emotion. Timothy held the apostle's heart; he was his son in the faith. This depth of affection heightens the pain of the apostle's goodbye.

Timothy and Paul had years of history together. The first recorded meeting of the two was when Paul came to Derbe and Lystra, an area in south-central Asia Minor where Paul traveled after intense persecution and stoning at the hands of angry Jews. Paul was immediately impressed with this young man's testimony among the believers and he therefore went to the necessary lengths to prepare him to join in his missionary journeys.[5] The New Testament is replete with mentions of this disciple, who joined Paul often on missionary travels, aided him in focused ministry, and served as a co-equal in the advancement of the Gospel. Timothy himself was imprisoned for his faith, and served to minister on Paul's behalf during his incarcerations. In this final letter Paul wrote to his beloved friend, he urged him for one last meeting.

Grace, Mercy, and Peace

Grace, mercy, and peace from God the Father and Christ Jesus our Lord.

2 TIMOTHY 2:2B

What is grace? It is God's kindness to undeserving sinners. It is His goodness and justice on full display. The Bible is explicit on the depravity of man, stating, "There is none righteous, not even one" (Romans 3:10b). But God's grace is the greatest outpouring of love imaginable—the crushing of His only Son as the perfect sacrifice for unworthy creatures, to bring them to Himself. God's grace is our only hope for salvation, as He is Holy and we are not.

And what is God's mercy? It is the benevolent heart position that God takes toward us. His grace is the action spurred by His mercy. It is the great eternal mystery that Paul references in the book of Romans, "So then it does not depend on the man who wills or the man who runs, but on God who has mercy" (Romans 9:16).

Peace is manifested through the outpouring of the Holy Spirit in the life of a regenerated believer. The original Greek word, *eirēnē,* carries the meaning of being tranquil, quiet, and at rest.[6] Grace, mercy, and peace are offered to the believer through Jesus Christ, and are only fully available in Him.

The gulf between these virtues and our culture is infinite. Rather than peace, our world offers us violence and innumerable factions between people. Instead of grace, we are faced with increasing hatred between political parties and irreconcilable differences between nations. Mercy is exchanged for a weaponized construct of "personal rights" which allows for many atrocities in the name of freedom. As mothers, we want to shield our little ones from these dangerous influences. Yet, despite our best efforts, we cannot create a utopia where they can be forever sheltered from a world that knows so little of grace, mercy, and peace. We would be naïve to believe such an existence was possible, and deluded to think this is as bad as the world ever has been, or ever could be.

Paul lived in just as dark an hour, and I feel certain that this is why he wrote such a powerful letter prior to his execution. He knew that for Timothy to continue in the faith might cost him a similar fate. In a world where hope seemed lost, he reminded Timothy of the eternal life that was their common joy in Christ. He greeted Timothy with grace, mercy, and peace, reminding him of these spiritual blessings that the Lord had made available to them and the body of Christ.

John MacArthur notes of this greeting, "Although commonly expressed as a greeting, these were not just words, but the expression of a genuine desire for God's best to be reality in the young preacher's life."[7] Paul understood that in difficult times, these were the gifts Timothy would need the most. Instead of trying to encourage Timothy with circumstantial change, he pointed him to the hope and promise of God. These gifts are from God for a heart fixed on God, expectant of His promises and His hope.

We Are Not the Kissing Sailor

It's easy to superimpose our life over what we read in Scripture and guess how our lives will work out. But we are not the kissing sailor. Many people have seen the famous *Kissing War Goodbye* print and imagined a story behind the image. But they have imagined incorrectly, without knowing the story behind the photograph.

We are not the artist painting the picture of our lives nor of our children's lives. As we walk through the seasons to which the Lord calls us, we must understand that sometimes we don't have all the information to truly grasp the context. However, Scripture does teach us to know and understand the heart of God, so we can be prepared for every good work[8] and so we can learn to trust Him more fully.

Likely none of us have been called to relate to Paul's experience, nor the impending loss that Timothy felt as he received this Epistle. Despite different circumstances, we can approach our lives knowing the Author of our lives is the same as the Author of Paul's life. The same hope he had in Christ can be ours. The same promise of eternal life can be ours. We too, can face bleak circumstances with grace, mercy, and peace. We can teach our children to walk into the world courageously because of these gifts afforded us through Christ Jesus our Lord.

How can you develop a culture of grace, mercy, and peace within your heart and home?

_____

_____

_____

_____

_____

_____

_____

TWO

SERVING FAITHFULLY AND CONTINUALLY

*I thank God, whom I serve with a clear conscience the
way my forefathers did, as I constantly remember you
in my prayers night and day, longing to see you, even
as I recall your tears, so that I may be filled with joy.*

2 TIMOTHY 1:3-4

MY ELDERLY GRANDPARENTS SAT in the guestroom
of their home. Married 67 years, their union was threatened by
the shadow of approaching death. Heart failure had claimed
his health, and in these final days, his mind slipped closer
to eternity. She helped make him comfortable, ensuring he
was securely seated on his bed. The air was thick with the
gravity of the moment. His days were few. Although she was
his caregiver, her own body had taken its toll with chronic
conditions and pain.

She wondered what her life would hold when he was no
longer there—how she would continue without him—though
she didn't voice these thoughts. Rather, just as she had the days
and months and years before, she opened her Bible and began

the morning reading. Her voice cracked a bit as parts of the passage seemed uniquely suited to their present circumstances, but she continued steadily on. He listened. It was a precious moment, infused with the sadness of physical loss and the triumph of heavenly hope.

A few weeks before my grandfather's home going, I visited him and witnessed this special time. The moment might have seemed ordinary as the two went about their daily routine. In fact, it was extraordinary. They were facing death and separation with steadfast hope and faithfulness. Witnessing my grandfather's final days was special—a testimony of the faithfulness of God lived out in a marriage filled with love and devotion.

Lately, faithfulness is a characteristic uncommon in our culture. Relationships are unmaintained, and rifts go unrepaired due to devalued faithfulness. And in a world without certainty, faithfulness is needed more than ever before. It is an anchor of security we are able to gift our children, and a way we are able to faintly image the character of God.

Serving with Gratitude

I thank God, whom I serve with a clear conscience the way my forefathers did, as I constantly remember you in my prayers night and day.

2 TIMOTHY 1:3

Paul concludes his greeting and moves into the meat of his message with two deeply encouraging truths. He, a man condemned to die, stood with a clear conscience before His God. He, a condemned prisoner in the worst of human conditions, remembered Timothy *constantly* and with *thanksgiving* in his prayers.

Gratitude graced Paul's life and his writing. In his letter to the Ephesian church, Paul wrote rejoicing of their fervent faith, stating that he did "*not cease giving thanks for you,* while making mention of you in my prayers" (Ephesians 1:16b). He reminded the church at Colossae to continue in the faith with gratitude when he wrote, "Therefore as you have received Christ Jesus the Lord, so walk in him...overflowing with gratitude" (Colossians 2:6-7b). Gratitude echoed in his words to the Thessalonians with his rapid-fire exhortations, "Rejoice always; pray without ceasing; in everything give thanks; for this is God's will for you in Christ Jesus" (1 Thessalonians 5:16-18). This final epistle also shines with this beautiful attribute. Paul remembered Timothy with gratitude, and this gratitude spurred him on to continual prayer. What an encouragement this news must have been to the young pastor and disciple of Christ.

For what reasons might have Paul given thanks for Timothy? Perhaps he was thankful for the ministry Timothy would continue in his absence. Maybe he was reminded of the many people they had served together, the hearts they had seen come to know the Lord, and he gave thanks that the Lord had used he and Timothy to build God's kingdom. Maybe he gave thanks for the friendship of a loving, compassionate soul who was a great comfort at a time of such isolation and difficulty. The text would suggest that he gave thanks for Timothy's affection for him as he recalled the young man's tears,[9] no doubt surrounding their parting. Paul was thankful that Timothy was a friend, one who cared and continued to care even in his hardest times. What an example of a heart set on the Lord.

As Nancy Leigh DeMoss puts it in *Choosing Gratitude,*

> "Gratitude is a lifestyle. A hard-fought, grace-infused, biblical lifestyle. And though there's a sense in which anyone can be thankful- for God has extended His common grace to all- the true glory and transforming power of gratitude are reserved for those who know and acknowledge the Giver of every good gift and who are recipients of His redeeming grace."

If any human had reason to be ungrateful, it seems circumstance would have deemed Paul exempt from gratitude. Yet this overflowing of the Holy Spirit enabled Paul to keep a heavenward focus.

How often do we model this sort of unconditional gratitude? Do we demonstrate this same type of thankfulness for the children that God has given us, or do we litter our conversations with complaining about their childish behavior and inconveniences? Do your children hear you complain? Do you talk to your friends about your children's shortcomings? There's no harm in brainstorming with your spouse about behavior problems, or troubleshooting how to help your three-year-old finish potty training, but keep in mind that complaining never helps. It merely sows the seeds of discontent, starting a vicious cycle of searching for the next milestone that hopefully brings relief. Like when your child sleeps through the night, learns to read and write, or is able to regulate their emotions.

Rather than giving thanks to God for the precious soul(s)

He has gifted us to raise and to mold, we complain which makes us wish away the very job we are called to complete. We are called to guide our children to Christlikeness. A heart devoid of gratitude can scarcely complete this calling.

What is the result of thanksgiving? In her book, *Secure in the Everlasting Arms*, Elisabeth Elliot explains it like this: "Thanksgiving brings contentment. Many people seem to be looking ceaselessly for amusement, for some alleviation from boredom. Dissatisfied and restless, they fritter away their lives, wishing to move from what or where they are to what or where they aren't."

We see the fruit of contentment in the life of Paul and in his letter to Timothy. He is focused on the well-being of his spiritual son, praying for him constantly, and remembering him in his prayers. He is not self-focused or lamenting his plight. He is filled with gratitude, and more than that, he is willing to articulate this thankfulness. That's spiritual strength!

Serving in Prayer

I thank God, whom I serve with a clear conscience the way my forefathers did, as I constantly remember you in my prayers night and day.

2 TIMOTHY 1:3B

How many of us mamas have started saving for our child's college fund? Not long ago I was visiting with a friend who was discussing her family's plan to better budget their finances. She mentioned several broad categories for saving, and then voiced the need for their family to begin saving for her daughters' college funds. I was taken aback. It hadn't occurred to me that I would have a budget for my kids' formula and diapers concurrent with their 529, but after researching it, I learned I was mistaken. Major researchers show that parents are wise to do so. With the average non-profit university posting tuition of close to $40k per year, financial experts suggest it is best to begin setting aside several hundred dollars a month for college when your child is only one year old.[10]

Not every parent deems college the best investment for their child's future. However, all good parents ensure their children are prepared to navigate transition between childhood and adulthood. This might come in the form of apprenticeships, work experience, or hobbies that will hone skills applicable to future jobs. We all want children who develop into confident, well-adjusted, capable men and women who are able to thrive in the world around them.

But as we shuffle them to violin lessons and soccer practice, do we remember their spiritual development? Do we prioritize their walk with the Lord above their SAT scores or their position in the honor society? Do we place value on our own prayer life for them, understanding the vital role our prayer ministry has in their future?

Alistair Begg writes in *Pray Big*, "To pray is an admission and an expression of dependence." Prayer is agreeing with God about who He is and who we are. It is confessing that we are dependent upon Him and it is a form of worship. Paul understood the value and necessity of prayer, often outlining his requests for the churches in his letters to them. Unlike our prayers, which are so often focused on the external, Paul prayed for the spiritual health of his friends. He asked God

to grow them into Christlikeness, reflected in his prayer for
the Ephesian church:

> "That He would grant you, according to the
> riches of His glory, to be strengthened with
> power through His Spirit in the inner man, so
> that Christ may dwell in your hearts through
> faith; and that you, being rooted and grounded
> in love, may be able to comprehend with all the
> saints what is the breadth and length and height
> and depth, and to know the love of Christ which
> surpasses knowledge, that you may be filled up
> to the fullness of God" (Ephesians 3:16-19).

What did Paul desire for the Ephesian church? Strengthening the inner man by the indwelling Spirit of Christ. That
they might understand in a deep, tangible way the love of
God. He further urged this church to pray at all times with all
persistence and all petition for all the saints. And for himself,
he asked the church to "pray on my behalf, that utterance
may be given to me in the opening of my mouth, to make
known with boldness the mystery of the gospel, for which
I am an ambassador in chains; that in proclaiming it I may
speak boldly, as I ought to speak" (Ephesians 6:19-20).

Note Paul's request, centered upon the furtherance of
the Gospel. Yes, he was suffering for the Gospel, but that
was not his concern. He wanted to see the Gospel advanced,
so his request was for boldness, rather than relief from his
circumstances.

What did Paul pray for his protégé in the faith? He was
offering prayers of gratitude to God. Much like his opening
greeting, Paul's desire and focus was for Timothy's spiritual

well-being. It isn't that Paul was unaware of Timothy's physical needs,[11] he just understood the preeminence of the Gospel and Timothy's important role in helping it to spread.

What a motivation truth must have been to Timothy! His mentor awaited certain death, yet rather than dwelling on circumstances, he was praying—*for him*. Charles Spurgeon comments, "At that time, Timothy was very specifically laid on the apostle's heart. He did not seem to think of anything without young Timothy's image raising up before him "night and day."[12]

Paul understood what mattered. His prayers spanned the future and sought the very best for Timothy. He wanted Timothy to participate in the furtherance of the Gospel.

In our home, we have chores we expect our children to complete before privileges like movies or other entertainment can be enjoyed. There have been times children have pushed aside practicing their instrument or cleaning their room in favor of what they felt in that moment to be more enjoyable. We have had conversations many times about not sacrificing the better choice for the easier choice. It's difficult to give up playing Legos to tidy a bedroom! But as parents, it is our job to help our children recognize how all actions play out with consequences, both good and bad. Similarly, Paul reminds Timothy to focus on the true reward of his faith. He encourages him with the reassurance of his prayers and his gratitude for him.

Serving with Affection

Longing to see you, even as I recall your
tears, so that I may be filled with joy.

2 TIMOTHY 1:4

Living in rural Texas has disadvantages; namely, poisonous spiders, rattlesnakes, and poor cellphone coverage. However, the advantages are plentiful. Breathtaking sunsets. Clerks who welcome you like a friend. And deer season. In central Texas, the opening day of deer season is second only to Christmas. The first weekend in November, our little grocery store is packed with camo-clad hunters, all bustling through the aisles looking for snacks for the next stint in the deer blind.

Late each fall, some of our close friends come to hunt and visit. This couple has been in ministry for years, and we treasure our lengthy conversations and fellowship with them between their hunting sessions. During the year, we long to see them and we relish the time together. Our desire to be with this couple is only a faint understanding of Paul's longing to be with Timothy.

Paul understood that his death was imminent, and so he urgently requested that Timothy come see him in prison. Three times in this short epistle he made mention of asking Timothy to visit him. And although Paul's focus was far from self-pity, we catch a glimpse of the apostle's humanity repeated in this request. Likely, he was deeply lonely and discouraged. Later in the epistle, Paul listed the many Christians who had deserted him, saying that only Luke was with him and that he had been completely abandoned at his trial.[13]

Paul didn't just pray for Timothy out of duty. He didn't

casually want to catch up with him either, to hear the latest gossip. This was a deep friendship, filled with love and affection. Timothy could not have doubted this love, and was only reaffirmed in Paul's moving letter.

As we mother our children, do we serve them like Paul served Timothy? Even in his final days, Paul was pouring humility, compassion, and wisdom into this young man with constant prayers and encouragement. From a pit in the ground, Paul was interceding for the spiritual well-being of his beloved son in the faith. He was rejoicing over God's goodness to Timothy. He was longing for fellowship with him, and expressing deep affection for him.

Are we this passionate? This intentional? Are our hearts overflowing with consistant gratitude for our children? Do we articulate our gratitude for them to God as well as to them? Do our children know we love them and desire to be with them?

We will do well to learn from Paul's urgency. We live in a dark time, and our children need mothers who understand the brevity of their influence and are willing to parent accordingly. We cannot parent with passivity. This is no time for sub-par mothering. Far more important than acquiring one more hobby or home organization skill, we must value praying for our children.

We need to cultivate relationships with them—authentic, tangible relationships built on communication and shared experiences. Our children should know we want to be with them. This means talking to them eye-to-eye, cellphones put away. It means choosing our words carefully, thoughtfully when saying our evening prayers. To act like what we say we believe in actually matters—because it does. To parent with faithfulness continually because it is what our children need from us.

Are you building deep relationships with your children? Do you know their deepest desires and fears?

_____

_____

_____

_____

_____

_____

_____

_____

_____

THREE

SERVING IN GOD'S STRENGTH

For I am mindful of the sincere faith within you, which first dwelt in your grandmother Lois and your mother Eunice, and I am sure that it is in you as well.

For this reason I remind you to kindle afresh the gift of God which is in you through the laying on of my hands.

2 TIMOTHY 1:5-6

IT'S AN OVERLY RELATABLE scenario: tired, stressed-out mom plus wild, rambunctious child (or children). Add crayon marks scribbled all over the walls or toys strewn throughout the living room, a late arrival to co-op, and binge eating ice cream late at night to cope with feelings of inadequacy. This could be a faith-based mom movie, or a weekend at your house.

We live in a culture that champions relatability and affirms that motherhood is an opportunity to fail frequently. We aren't challenged to excellence, or to develop the fruit of the Spirit, but rather to live life alongside the little people we call our children while we all seek our own comfort and happiness.

But what about those moms in history who lived differently—who mothered in God's strength? What about Hannah, a righteous woman who dedicated her child to the Lord before he was born, and then left him in the care of the High Priest as a young child? Or Susanna Wesley, mother of two world-renowned pastors who spent multiple hours a day in the Word and prayer while raising and educating 10 children? What about American missionary Elisabeth Elliot, who raised her only daughter in the jungles of Ecuador, and ministered to a tribe who murdered her husband?

These are strangely unrelatable scenarios, and seem foreign because so seldom do we live in the strength that God has provided for us. Mothering in God's strength isn't an add-on to our daily routines or one more task to complete. Being empowered by the Holy Spirit is a humble dependency upon God's strength to accomplish His purposes. It is a mighty thing indeed.

In his letter to Timothy, Paul encouraged the young pastor to remember the strength that was his in Christ. Paul was clearly concerned that Timothy's passion for the Gospel was cooling, and therefore he reminded him of his *heritage* of his faith, the *commissioning* of his faith, and the *quality* of his faith. He reminded him of the unquenchable power of being indwelt by the Holy Spirit, and within this context he encouraged the young preacher to keep on keeping on, with passion and purpose. His faith was to be strong and disciplined, not for the sake of just barely making it through the day, but for the sake of serving the body of Christ and building God's kingdom.

A Heritage of Faith

For I am mindful of the sincere faith within you,
which first dwelt in your grandmother Lois and your
mother Eunice, and I am sure that it is in you as well.

2 TIMOTHY 1:5

Familiarity ingrains normalcy. Normalcy breeds unawareness and subconscious expectation. Perhaps your childhood family watched television every night. Likely your subconscious expected this method of relaxation after a hectic day, and still does. Your habits might be benign, like expecting coffee every morning or keeping your freezer stocked with your favorite ice cream. These habits tend to develop in our formative years, and have deep staying power. They open doors to personality traits, and offer landmarks of familiarity in our too-busy lives.

Generational repetitions are inherently neutral, but consider the value of a heritage of faith.

Paul reminded Timothy that he had the happy privilege of having a mother and grandmother who knew Jesus personally. This served only to benefit him in his ministry. Timothy had women who had invested in him spiritually from his youngest days, referenced by Paul later in the epistle, when he writes, "You, however, continue in the things you have learned and become convinced of, knowing from whom you have learned them, and that from childhood you have known the sacred writings which are able to give you the wisdom that leads to salvation through faith which is in Christ Jesus" (2 Timothy 3:14-15). And while Scripture does not indicate that Timothy's father was a believer (Acts 16:1), his mother and grandmother had been diligent to disciple Timothy in the faith.

Mamas, pause for a moment to reflect. What might the early church have looked like if Eunice and Lois had not been faithful to teach Timothy the Word? Paul wouldn't have had the assistance in his missionary journeys that Timothy provided, and our Bible would be missing two books. Who knows how many souls this man won to the Lord, and the wealth of other eternal fruit that his life brought for the Kingdom of God. These two godly women clearly took their call to disciple young Timothy seriously.

Good things take work. Clean laundry never happens by accident. People don't inadvertently get fit. Spiritual growth and discipleship are always intentional. We are commanded by Jesus to make disciples of all nations[14] and this begins with our children. We need to train our children to understand the Gospel and its doctrine. This means knowing the uncomfortable "whys?" of Scripture.

For example, why would a loving God strike a man dead just for touching the Ark? What is the erotic language found in Song of Solomon doing in the Bible? What is predestination and what is its importance? These aren't questions we need to address with our preschooler, but we also can't ignore the younger years as a time for important training in the Word. As our kids grow, our discussions of doctrine need to develop with them. Mamas, we need to be theologians so we can help our children thoroughly comprehend their faith. We *want* them coming to us with their questions.

What does that look like? It looks like effort. It requires humility and prayer, seeking to learn and grow in our personal walk with the Lord. It looks like researching age-appropriate resources for training little ones in God's Word. It requires a plan for follow-through. It might include listening to an audio-bible with your kids on the way to school, and discussing what you learned on the way home. Maybe you spend Sunday nights cuddled up on the couch with hot cocoa, working through the Gospels. Perhaps your children are grown, yet you engage them in an online study through a Bible app. What you do is going to depend greatly on your schedule and the season of mothering you are in. But the important thing is that you make the effort to intentionally integrate Scripture into your child's everyday life.

In *Mama Bear Apologetics* by Hillary Morgan Ferrer, the author writes,

> "The Mama Bear realizes her life on Earth is finite, and she wants to make it purposeful. She knows her legacy is not wrapped up in the jewelry and china she passes down, but in the pearls of wisdom and character she gifts her children. She admits when she lacks the answer, yet is willing to search for it. She corrects course and mends fences when she has erred in fact, tone or deed. Above all, she recognizes the dignity in the questioner behind the question because she loves others as God's creatures."

Celebrate the little victories as you progress in growing a culture of faith in your home. Cherish the moments your child makes a connection in church with something you said about the Bible. When your two-year-old asks to pray, listen eagerly and praise them for their efforts. Make devotions expected and even eagerly anticipated by your children. Create opportunities for rich, intentional conversations about the things of God. Let these spiritual habits be a foundational component of your home, and a priceless cornerstone to your child's spiritual heritage.

A Commissioning of Faith

For this reason I remind you to kindle afresh the gift of God which is in you through the laying on of my hands.

2 TIMOTHY 1:6

In our home, we love candles. Most every afternoon I spend a portion of my youngest daughter's naptime with a cup of coffee, reading material, and a scented candle. My children understand my affinity for this luxury, and have inherited my "gene" for stopping in the grocery store or Dollar Store to peruse the shelves for the best candle flavors. This winter, however, my son developed a helpful habit of walking around and blowing out candles that he finds unattended. If I am not actively protecting the flickering flame, he leans over and extinguishes it like he's practicing for his next birthday cake. They don't stand a chance.

There's little value in a candle that has been extinguished. It lets off no heat. It gives no light. The only way it can be made valuable again, is to have a match reignite the wick. This is the image Paul uses when he exhorts Timothy to remain devoted to the faith. Rekindle!

The Greek lexicon for this word explains it as, "the remains of a fire, embers;" or "that by which the fire is kindled anew or lighted up, a pair of bellows."[15] These are the tiny glowing coals of a bonfire the morning after a gathering. They still hold potential for fire, but they have already served their usefulness. This leftover glow is not what Paul wanted for

Timothy. This particular choice of words gives us a glimpse into perhaps why Timothy was the recipient of Paul's last letter. Paul's first epistle to Timothy jumps straight from greetings to swift exhortations about Church leadership and warnings against factitious doctrines. However, this epistle is different. Paul reminds Timothy of his spiritual heritage, and to rekindle his faith.

Was Paul concerned that Timothy's faith was being extinguished? In his final days, this aged apostle gave several strong reminders to the young preacher. He told him not to be ashamed of the testimony of the Lord, encouraged him to be strong, to continue in the things he had learned, and to preach the Word.[16] He also admonished Timothy regarding the commissioning of his faith.

It seems that the commissioning of Timothy must have been a spiritual high for the young man. The first epistle bearing his name mentions "prophecies previously made concerning you" (1 Timothy 1:18). The Bible teacher, John MacArthur explains, "These prophecies specifically and supernaturally called Timothy into God's service."[17] In the same letter, Paul also encourages Timothy not to neglect his spiritual gift, writing, "which was bestowed on you through prophetic utterance with the laying on of hands by the presbytery" (1 Timothy 4:14). It seems the time that Timothy was called into the ministry was a season rich with confirmation and Spirit-enabled influence. Timothy was chosen to serve alongside Paul, commissioned to a position of power. What a miraculous time this must have been. However, the days of joy-filled service had come to an end, stymied by Nero's fierce persecution of the Christians.

No doubt Paul recognized or predicted Timothy's fear and

discouragement. So he used the proverbial "bellows" in pen and ink to evoke Timothy to remain faithful. He rehearsed with Timothy the history of his commissioning. His heritage. He didn't reprimand Timothy for any wavering in the faith, but in his final days, he worked to breathe life into this pastor, speaking encouragement and hope.

Perhaps some of you mamas or grandmothers have a child in the same place as Timothy. Maybe you see them wavering or even shrinking back from their faith. You have the special opportunity to be their bellows. You can be the gentle reminder of God's faithfulness to them. Now let's try putting the shoe on a different foot. Perhaps you're the person feeling that your season of ministry has come to an end. Maybe you are in the twilight years of your life, and lack the physical strength to serve as you once did. Consider Paul's situation in the writing of this letter. He scarcely had a possession to his name. He was a condemned man, and his influence was ebbing. He was elderly and lacked the basic necessities of sanitation and privacy. Yet in these final days in such uncongenial surroundings, he busied himself with continual prayer and one final letter of encouragement. It seems unlikely the apostle could have ever imagined the scope of impact this last letter would carry, or the billions of lives it would eventually change. He was simply being obedient to the leading of the Holy Spirit.

My dear friend, do not despise the small things.

You may not be in a season where you have a large platform or a commanding presence. That's okay. Be faithful in the little things. You can pray. You can encourage. You can point those around you to the Word. You are building the Kingdom of God through your obedience to the Lord's calling on your life. Your ministry might focus solely on little ones as you help them potty train, or minister to your adult children who come to mow your lawn. In whatever your circumstance, in whatever your station, do your part to rekindle that flame that needs your wisdom and inspiration.

How can you cultivate an atmosphere that encourages spiritual growth in your home?

_____

_____

_____

_____

_____

_____

_____

FOUR

THE QUALITY OF FAITH

For God has not given us a spirit of timidity,
but of power and love and discipline.

2 TIMOTHY 1:7

THERE ARE TWO TYPES of people who drink coffee. There are those who love the taste. Connoisseurs who find comparing single origin coffees both intellectually stimulating as well as culturally enriching. They purchase all the tools to grind and roast their coffee to achieve maximal flavor and freshness for their drink. With great care, they measure the beans, boil the water, and prepare the perfect cup. They drink their coffee slowly, thoughtfully, giving full attention to the bouquet of aromas and flavors while savoring each drop. They drink coffee because they love it! It is an art. An experience. A luxury.

Then there's the other group of coffee drinkers. They are practical, go to the supermarket and buy the cheapest pre-ground coffee they can find. They pre-program their coffee-maker so when they stumble out of bed in the morning, they are greeted by a steaming, strong cup of Joe. These people drink coffee because they require caffeine to function.

Although both groups of people would call themselves coffee drinkers, the quality of their experience is drastically different. My point: *quality matters.*

Paul led up to this point when reminding Timothy of the heritage of his faith—a privileged boy having been discipled by two godly, devoted family members. He reminded Timothy of the commissioning of his faith and the unique milestones in his life that had culminated in his ordination as a pastor. More important than these snapshots of the past, Paul helped Timothy remember the quality of his faith—not something used up or no longer needed, but rather living, active, and necessary in the present. Timothy was empowered by the Holy Spirit, and he needed to internalize that truth for his future as a leader in Paul's absence.

This verse starts with a profound negative statement: "For God has not given us a spirit of timidity."

Paul knows that God is the giver of every good and perfect gift.[18] Always. Therefore, he begins this verse by reminding Timothy (and us) that the good gifts he has received are from the Lord. Specifically, the gift of the Holy Spirit.

Jesus had predetermined for believers, that He would send the Holy Spirit; a Helper and a Guide to the world, to aid them.[19] The Spirit referenced by Paul is the same word used to describe the third person of the Godhead—who allowed the virgin Mary to conceive and give birth to Jesus.[20] He was active in the life and ministry of Jesus Christ, manifesting Himself as a dove at the baptism of Jesus[21] and directing Jesus' work throughout His earthly ministry.[22]

Times were tough, and no doubt Timothy needed reassuring of the quality of his faith. God had equipped him with what he needed to faithfully serve Him. He was strengthened by the Holy Spirit in order to serve God free from fear. These verses echo the promise in the prophecy of Zachariah, shortly after John the Baptist's birth. He said,

> *"Blessed be the Lord God of Israel,*
>
> *For He has visited us and*
> *accomplished redemption for His people,*
>
> *And has raised up a horn of salvation for us*
>
> *In the house of David His servant—*
>
> *To grant us that we, being rescued from*
> *the hand of our enemies,*
>
> *Might serve Him without fear,*
>
> *In holiness and righteousness before Him all our days."*

LUKE 1:68-69, 74-75

In Timothy's world, imprisonment and execution were not theoretical scenarios for Christ followers. Timothy was being tutored in the nature of the Spirit within him, and the divine resources already made available to him in Christ. Likely he was afraid, perhaps discouraged or depressed. Why else would Paul go to such great lengths to encourage and exhort this pastor? Timothy needed to stay grounded in the past in order to move fearlessly in his present position as an ambassador of Jesus Christ.

How do we draw application from Paul's mentorship in the context in which we mother? How do we fill the "Paul" role for our children, helping them remember the Gospel and understand the staying power that it has for their lives? How do we mother in God's strength and help our little ones to understand the transformative work of the Gospel and the Holy Spirit?

We can only show what we know.

Perhaps the first thing we need as mamas is to be reminded of our own position in Christ, remembering the faithfulness that God has shown to us. We need to understand the riches of His kindness, and how in Christ we have everything we require for life and godliness.[23] This is really hard to wrap our heads around, especially in a season where it's tough to just keep kids in clean clothes and have groceries in the fridge. How are we supposed to also find time to meditate on the Lord?

We do it by creating margin in our lives. We do it by extending grace to ourselves—knowing that we need not do everything perfectly. But we *must* seek the Lord well. Perhaps the season of motherhood in which you are living right now requires near insurmountable effort to keep your home running smoothly, your children growing safely, and your marriage thriving effectively. I have three words for you:

Outsource.

Simplify.

Release.

Outsource those things others can help with. Simplify tasks that don't require perfection—that's a lot of them. And release your expectations for a tidy home or daily workouts or your children participating in multiple extra-curriculars so that you can find the space to rest.

The quality of your faith dictates your capacity to mother well. Cherish your walk with the Lord. Seek Him, and watch your capacity to love well be transform as you learn to mother in His strength.

Do you cherish your walk with the Lord and is it the source of your daily strength? What steps can you take to make it stronger?

_____

_____

_____

_____

_____

_____

_____

FIVE

MOTHERING WITH COURAGE

Therefore do not be ashamed of the testimony of our Lord or of me His prisoner, but join with me in suffering for the gospel according to the power of God, who saved us and called us with a holy calling, nor according to our works, but according to His own purpose and grace which was granted us in Christ Jesus from all eternity, but now been revealed by the appearing of our Savior Christ Jesus, who abolished death and brought life and immortality to light through the gospel, for which I was appointed a preacher and a teacher. For this reason, I also suffer these things, but I am not ashamed.

2 TIMOTHY 1:8-12A

IN 2002, WERNER GROENEWALD and his wife, Hannelie, felt the Lord calling them to serve as missionaries in Afghanistan. They had concerns about this move. Afghanistan had been the origin of the terrorists who attacked the New York Twin Towers only months before. They had two young children at the time. What were the risks that they could be killed? The writer of their story shared their final decision to move: "They trusted the Lord, knowing His call was just as real as the dangers they might face, and they knew that obedience to God mattered more than their fears."[24]

Eleven years into their ministry, the Groenewald family had navigated the culture shock and settled into their lives in Afghanistan. Werner served with several humanitarian organizations, and helped with teaching leadership and English. Hannelie served as a doctor at a nearby clinic.

One day, while she was at a meeting, three armed men attacked the compound where the family lived, murdering Werner and their two children. Later, Hannelie commented on the loss of her family; "We had a clear calling...We had a mandate with this; we counted the cost. We knew that something like this could happen. God allowed that for a reason."[25]

This is courage—to be obedient to God regardless of the cost. It is doing the hard thing even when you are afraid. In his letter to Timothy, Paul called for this same courage at a time when following Christ could cause very real danger. "Therefore do not be ashamed of the testimony of our Lord or of me His prisoner, but join with me in suffering for the gospel according to the power of God" (2 Timothy 1:8).

Paul wasn't calling Timothy to an unfamiliar lifestyle. When Paul was first converted, the Lord prophesied that he would suffer, and that was no idle threat.[26] In his second letter to the Corinthian church, Paul outlined an overview of these trials he had faced for Christ. Service to Jesus had cost him repeated beatings, exposure to death, a stoning, a shipwreck, and a transient lifestyle. Danger. Exhaustion. Nakedness. Hunger. Mental and emotional pressure investing in the churches.[27] All of these perils Paul withstood without hesitation or complaint. Yet he knew that the pain he endured was well worth the cost. It was because of his confidence in the surpassing value of the Gospel that he could encourage Timothy to join with him. Not just in sharing the Gospel, but in *suffering* for it.

Elisabeth Elliot, missionary to a people who murdered her husband, commented on this subject when she stated; "And let's never forget that if we don't ever want to suffer, we must be very careful never to love anything or anybody."[28]

Love for Christ requires exposing ourselves to challenges. Jesus told His followers to expect no less.[29] Loving Christ means counting the cost, as Paul clearly set the example. Timothy, as well. For us to mother with courage, we must be willing to wrap our minds around this truth—that discipleship will cost us. We accept this truth confident that Christ is worth any sacrifice.

Paul offered this exhortation and also hope of the strengthening of God's Spirit in us for every challenge we face. "Therefore do not be ashamed of the testimony of our Lord or of me His prisoner, but join with me in suffering for the gospel according to the power of God" (2 Timothy 1:8). Jesus brought up a similar warning during His time on earth, stating that those who were ashamed of Him, He would be ashamed of before His Father.[30]

But there is hope. Paul's admonition to Timothy is ours, as well. We are to prepare for suffering, to anticipate it rather than dread it. But we also are to be encouraged that Christ has not only promised suffering, but also sure victory through His work on the Cross. In some of His final words to His disciples, He offered this encouragement, "These things I have spoken to you, so that in Me you may have peace. In the world you have tribulation, but take courage; I have overcome the world" (John 16:33).

So how do we process these verses? We anticipate hardship. And we take courage.

Remember the Gospel

Paul didn't simply remind Timothy to anticipate suffering as if being a Christian was a masochistic call to martyrdom. He pointed him to the value of the Gospel, the eternal treasure that was theirs already in Christ. He reminded Timothy that it was God:

> "Who saved us and called us with a holy calling, nor according to our works, but according to His own purpose and grace which was granted us in Christ Jesus from all eternity, but now been revealed by the appearing of our Savior Christ Jesus, who abolished death and brought life and immortality to light through the gospel. For which I was appointed a preacher and a teacher. For this reason, I also suffer these things, but I am not ashamed" (2 Timothy 1:9-12a).

Paul reminded Timothy that the Gospel was their hope, their identity, and their future. God had shown them mercy through sending His only Son to die for their sins.[31] This glorious heritage was well worth the sacrifice.[32]

We need to live like conquerors. We do this by rehearsing the Gospel and communicating its value to our family and friends. We do this by growing thick skin and accepting ridicule and name-calling for the sake of our faith. We do this by having a singular focus on what Christ has done for us, and allowing our lives to truly center on this truth.

This also means that we live out the calling God has placed on our lives. Maybe some of you are stay-at-home mothers and you struggle with insecurity being "just a mom" rather than having a paid vocation. Maybe God never gave you biological children, but you have a burden for teens in your community to be discipled in the Word. Perhaps you are in a traditional office setting and don't have access to youth in any way, but the Lord keeps bringing a younger believer across your path during your lunch hour.

Living out your calling as a Christ-follower looks different for everyone, but it always requires obedience, using the very best you have as an offering to the Lord. Obedience might mean starting a Bible study with a coworker. You might ask the Lord to give you a settled heart in a season where you are not bringing in an income. Maybe obedience to Christ asks you to join a teen ministry with your local parachurch organization so you can reach kids at the local high school.

Jesus declares openly that following Him requires sacrifice, as He explains to His disciples in the Book of Matthew: "If anyone wishes to come after Me, he must deny himself, and take up his cross and follow Me. For whoever wishes to save his life will lose it; but whoever loses his life for My sake will find it" (Matthew 16:24b-25). Obedience requires self-denial. It means giving Jesus absolutely everything you have and letting Him handle the results.

Mothering with courage means understanding the reality of trouble here in this world, but it also means celebrating the overwhelming worth of the Gospel. It means that anything we are called to give up, is well worth it. It means our lives are marked by obedience to Jesus, and this obedience gives our actions value and purpose. Our kids need to see this. They need moms who aren't listless, looking for fulfillment through shopping or networking or endless personal growth. Our kids need moms who understand with their head and heart what the Lord has called them to, and are committed in that calling. They need mothers who are calm and confident, unshaken by the latest conspiracy theory or legitimate threat. Moms who understand and accept that suffering is real, but the Gospel is worth it. Our children need moms that mother with courage.

Think of a sacrifice the Lord might be asking you to make to mother courageously. What might that look like?

_____

_____

_____

_____

_____

_____

SIX

MOTHERING WITH CONFIDENCE

*For I know whom I have believed, and I am
convinced that He is able to protect what I
have entrusted to Him until that day.*

2 TIMOTHY 1:12B

WE LIVE IN A world devoid of absolutes. This translates to all aspects of life, but is especially relevant to the world of mothering. How often have you heard moms discussing their position on childbirth or vaccinations or breastfeeding only to qualify their stance with the phrase, "But no judgement..." We live in a society where the cardinal sin is intolerance. We desire, more than being a godly mother, to be a tolerant one. In this quest for tolerance, do we lose the capacity to mother with confidence?

Despite how culture might fight it, there *are* absolutes. Seasons follow predictable patterns. Gravity remains constant. The sun exists, and we feel its warmth, benefit from its light, and depend on it for our very lives. Apart from order and reason, our world would be uninhabitable. Stating that we don't believe in order and the intelligent design of our universe doesn't change its reality or our dependence upon it.

Similarly, our acknowledgement of the reality of God does not alter who He is or His reality in our lives. It does, however, diametrically impact our capacity to mother with confidence.

Paul understood the importance of planting his flag in the reality and relevance of the Gospel. This was more than just speech; his belief in the exclusivity of the Gospel dictated his every action. With utter confidence, Paul was able to say, "for I know whom I have believed, and I am convinced that He is able to protect what I have entrusted to Him until that day."

Paul was convinced in Christ enough to face hardship for the Gospel. Convinced enough to follow Christ into the darkest of places. Convinced enough to give up his own life in obedience.

Convinced in *Who*, not *What*

Paul's perfect confidence was in the person of Jesus Christ and the nature of God. From the moment of his conversion, Paul was given insight into who Jesus was (and is), and that being called by Him would require a radical transformation of his life.[33] Conversion for Paul meant a change in identity, a change in vocation, and a complete transformation of lifestyle.

Before Paul knew Jesus, he was a violent persecutor of Christians. He was a Pharisee, a teacher to the Jews, and established with an enviable political and social position of power. But his Damascus Road encounter with Jesus demanded that all of this change. Paul's conversion was irrefutable. His traveling companions heard the voice of Christ, although they saw no one.[34] Blinded by the light from heaven, Paul spent three days in darkness, until Ananias, one of the leaders in the local church, was called by the Lord in a vision to come restore Paul's sight to him.[35] Immediately, Paul was a changed man—to the anger of the Jewish leaders and the confusion of the Christians—suddenly and boldly preaching the truth of the Gospel that he had been so intent to destroy. It was not until one of the disciples, a man named Barnabas, was willing to vouch for the veracity of Paul's conversion that the disciples were able to accept him as a true believer.[36]

Paul's conversion meant a change in his nature and in his spiritual purpose. He had unwavering confidence in the person of Jesus Christ and the things He had taught him. Paul was completely transformed. Minister and author John MacArthur writes,

> "The object of Paul's certain knowledge was not a thing, or even God's truth, as important as it is, but rather God Himself. It was not Paul's divinely revealed theology, but the One who revealed to him that theology, in whom he believed. He was, in John's words, a spiritual father who had come to know the Eternal One (1 John 2:14)."[37]

Paul comforted Timothy by saying that despite his desperate physical situation in prison, his confidence in the person and purpose of Jesus had not changed. Paul knew Jesus. He understood that whatever happened to him, would only be allowed through the will of God. "I know whom I have believed," Paul stated. He knew that his confidence was in the person of *Jesus*, and the promise of eternal life that He had secured for him by His death on the Cross. This intimacy with Jesus sustained Paul in his moment of deepest need, and gave him confidence to face his future with peace and certainty.

A Convincing Character

Perhaps the most difficult thing about online dating is that often, people don't accurately represent themselves. With the use of photo filters, people present themselves as thinner, younger, and more blemish-free than they are in real life. Their character flaws can be sidestepped through carefully navigating uncomfortable questions in a chat bar. They can lie about their job, their relationship history, and their finances. Behind the safety of a screen, character is easily forged.

However, there is something about meeting a person face-to-face that forces facades to crumble. No matter how much makeup you apply or doctor your online profile, you alone defend your personality, mannerisms, and likability. You must own your character to gain closeness with another person.

Paul knew the character of Christ. Before his conversion, Paul had heard the claims of Jesus through His followers, yet he remained callous toward their belief of His deity. It was not until Jesus personally revealed Himself that Paul received the ability to accept the Good News of Salvation. Paul seems to have never lost sight of God's grace to him, as evidenced in his letter to the Corinthian church.

> "And last of all, as to one untimely born, He appeared to me also. For I am the least of the apostles, and not fit to be called an apostle, because I persecuted the church of God. But by the grace of God I am what I am, and His grace toward me did not prove vain" (1 Corinthians 15:8-10a).

Paul believed Christ's goodness to him, saving him from his sins. He came to terms with his own depravity and how much he didn't deserve the grace of God. He also accepted God's grace with his head and his heart, and from this confidence he was able to write in his great treatise to the Roman church.

> "For I am convinced that neither death, nor life, nor angels, nor principalities, nor things present, nor things to come, nor powers, nor height, nor depth, nor any other created thing will be able to separate us from the love of God that is in Christ Jesus our Lord" (Romans 8:38-39).

These were not mere words to Paul. He was convinced. Through the divine leading of the Holy Spirit, he crafted this letter, and communicate with painstaking clarity the confidence he had in his Savior.

This original Greek word for "convinced" that he uses is peithō, and carries with it the meaning to persuade or to induce one by words to believe. It is the same word Paul uses in his second epistle to Timothy, "For I know whom I have believed, and I am *convinced*." Peithō. Again, in his letter to the Philippian church he writes, "For I am *confident* of this very thing, that He who began a good work in you will perfect it until the day of Christ Jesus" (Philippians 1:6).

Don't confuse this repetition for mere semantics. Paul was a very learned man, and had command of an extensive vocabulary. But he chose this word to communicate something very important. He was steadfast. The Gospel was it. Jesus was it. Paul knew, and he was never going to back down from this truth. He had confidence in the character and nature of Christ.

Convinced in His Future

Death is one of the great certainties of life. As Paul wrote this letter to Timothy, he stared death in the face. He knew that the only way out of his prison cell was execution, and likely a brutal one at that. His seasons of fruitful ministry—times of deep fellowship and successful evangelism—had come to an end. He didn't have future missionary trips to plan, or young converts to disciple. As he stated later in the Epistle, "For I am already being poured out as a drink offering, and the time of my departure has come" (2 Timothy 4:6). And yet, in circumstances that should have given him every reason for earthly despair, he wrote words of confidence and peace.

Paul prepared to die with a calm heart. Although he still had great affection for Timothy, he didn't presume that Timothy *needed* him to continue in the faith. He didn't look at the proverbial fire and brimstone raining down on Rome in the form of a wicked ruler, and fret about the future of the Christian church. He didn't wonder if the Good News of Jesus would be extinguished by persecution. Rather, he was confident that the good work of the Gospel would be brought to completion by the power of Jesus Christ. He understood Him to be trustworthy, and recognized that he was only to play a part in the building of Christ's kingdom.

Paul's part had come to an end, and he was able to accept that. He was convinced in the reality of the Gospel and the glorious future that was his in Christ Jesus. Heaven waited him; Jesus would take care of His church. Of these things Paul was certain.

Do we mother with this same conviction? Do we trust that Jesus is sufficient to protect what we have entrusted to Him—our children or legacy? For many, this question becomes more difficult depending on what season of our life we are in. From a season of health and youth we can easily say, "Yeah, sure, Jesus will keep my children in His care." We say it because we imagine our death to be somewhere in the distant future, and our time with our children to be lengthy. But do we believe this when we face a terminal diagnosis? Do we internalize this truth and respond with a quiet heart when we face empty-nesting, or governmental upheaval, or worldwide unrest?

If the answer is no, perhaps we do not truly know the Who that we claim to believe in. Intimacy with Christ is the only rest our souls can find. As we grow in fellowship with the One in whom we believe, we grow to mother in confidence.

Do you have full confidence that the Lord will work His perfect purpose for your children even after you are gone? What feeds this confidence?

_____

_____

_____

_____

_____

SEVEN

MOTHERING WITH COMPETENCE

Retain the standard of sound words which you have heard from me, in the faith and love which are in Christ Jesus. Guard, through the Holy Spirit who dwells in us, the treasure which has been entrusted to you.

2 TIMOTHY 1:13-14

IF YOU WERE EVER a part of the little-league baseball world, you likely have a strong reaction to the words "pitching machine." For those of you who were athletically prone, the methodical exercise of hitting ball after ball likely came with some sense of deep satisfaction, and maybe even a little fist pumping in the dugout. However, for everyone else, pitching machines meant a non-stop onslaught of balls seeming to torpedo everywhere except your bat. Pitching machines are relentless, calculated, and if used long enough, a source of utter exhaustion.

Sometimes motherhood feels no different. It runs the gamut from MMA referee to private investigator, searching for that ever-elusive missing cleat or matching sock. It is a constant managing of material needs while simultaneously nurturing minds and cultivating hearts. It is an all-encompassing, never-ending task. And as Christ-following mothers, the call to disciple our little ones outstrips any other demand on our time or attention.

In the book *Mama Bear Apologetics*, Hillary Morgan Ferrer writes,

> "When spiritual questions are asked, they are likely being fielded by mom. For that reason, alone moms will end up doing apologetics the most! You are your family's front-line defense... Moms can have a profound influence on their children's spiritual development."

How often do these questions seem to come at you much like a pitching machine? *How do I know the Bible is true?* Whoosh. A ball flies by, unanticipated. *My teacher said evolution is real. You said God created the world.* Whoosh. *Why can't we watch that movie? Everyone else does.* Whoosh. How do we field these life-altering questions? How do we engage our children with confidence in a world that is constantly de-valuing the worth and inerrancy of Scripture? For answers, we go to the Bible itself.

Adhering to the Pattern

Paul points to the answer for these questions with the succinct instructions given to Timothy. "Retain the standard of sound words which you have heard from me, in the faith and love which are in Christ Jesus" (2 Timothy 1:13).

This original word that Paul employs, hypotypōsis, means

an outline, sketch, example or pattern.[38] Those who have experience in sewing or quilt making learned the value of adhering to a pattern. Without measuring and cutting *just so*, a pattern's result is a completely useless article of clothing. Similarly, aviation experts explain that "for every one degree a plane gets off course, it will miss its targeted landing spot by 92 feet for every mile you fly."[39] For lengthy flights, the consequences for such a seemingly small error can be dire.

In Paul's day, what were the ramifications for not holding onto the pattern of sound words? In many ways, the implications are no different now than they were then. As a teacher of the Word to an infant church, Timothy's job held great weight, and in his last days, Paul took great pains to remind Timothy to faithfully keep on teaching the word. This command seems a succinct repetition of his exhortation to Timothy in his earlier epistle:

> "Do not neglect the spiritual gift within you, which was bestowed on you through prophetic utterance with the laying on of hands by the presbytery. Take pains with these things; be absorbed in them, so that your progress will be evident to all. Pay close attention to yourself and to your teaching; persevere in these things, for as you do this you will ensure salvation both for yourself and for those who hear you" (1 Timothy 4:14-16).

Timothy was to strive to become a competent, capable teacher. He was to progress in gaining skill in his knowledge and handling of the Word. This was his vocation as well as his unique gifting by the Lord. In his encouragement, Paul also held Timothy accountable.

While we as mamas are not vocational teaching pastors, we, like Timothy, have a flock that we need to constantly care for. It is our duty to grow and develop in our knowledge of the Word not only for our own personal walks with the Lord, but so we can competently "field" the questions our children face daily. Aspire to be proactive, not simply reactive.

Mothers, be competent in articulating your faith, especially the Gospel. It is important that we understand what predestination is and what we believe about the end times. We need the skills to explore difficult passages in Scripture to discover why the God of the Old Testament and the God of the New Testament are the very same. Though His actions are the same, they may appear to look different after the Incarnation. Our working knowledge of what is in Scripture (and why) will serve us as mothers and mentors.

Evangelist Larry Moyer summarized the simplicity of the Gospel message by pointing to 1 Corinthians 15:3-5. This passage reads, "For I delivered to you as of first importance what I also received, that Christ died for our sins according to the Scriptures, and that He was buried, and that He was raised on the third day according to the Scriptures and that He was seen by Cephas, then by the twelve."

In his book, *101 Tips for Evangelism*, Moyer goes on to write, "So the Gospel can be reduced to ten words: 'Christ died for our sins and rose from the dead.' That is the message we have for unbelievers. That is what God calls, 'the power God to salvation for everyone who believes'" (Romans 1:16).[40]

Anyone can learn and articulate the saving message of Jesus, and every mama should. Understanding and being able to articulate orthodoxy is as necessary a skill set for a mother, as much as changing diapers or teaching our teen to drive. Our children need us to be competent in our handling of the Word of God. If we aren't able to handle their questions, be assured they will ask someone else. Do you want that on your conscience?

What a joy if we are prepared, though! What an amazing opportunity we have to disciple our kids, to teach them God's Word, and to learn all about what truly matters right alongside them. It is a huge task, but so worth the effort. Mamas, we do not want to relinquish this responsibility because we neglect learning God's Word for ourselves.

In the Faith and Love Which Are in Christ Jesus

Some things you best not muscle through. A runner wouldn't "wing it" for a marathon. A CEO wouldn't walk into a financial briefing for his business without reviewing the company's performance. A bride wouldn't fritter away the months before her wedding without working through the many details of her big day. People understand the need for preparation, yet all too often, this doesn't translate to our experience as mothers.

Too many moms spend their mothering career unprepared for the next challenge, and unequipped for the current struggle. They start each day exhausted from the night before, and push through the hours on too short a quiet time and too much coffee. They hope that they won't melt down when their toddler pees their pants one too many times, or when they face one too many surly comments from an older child. In their hearts, they know they don't look just like Christ, but they hope that they're getting close enough.

And yet the key to Christ-like and victorious living is in a little verse we might be tempted to skim past, "do so with the faith and love that are in Christ Jesus."[41] We are not called to be supermoms. We are not asked to live up to some impossible standard that we can never attain. We are called to be true to the Word of God, to steward His Words and His Gospel through the faith and love *in Him.* God provides His strength to accomplish His purposes so we can reflect *His* glory. This should get us excited!

Paul gives a fantastic visual for living this out in his letter to the Roman church. He writes, "But put on the Lord Jesus Christ, and make no provision for the flesh in regard to *its* lusts" (Romans 13:14).

How do we live in the faith and love found only in Christ Jesus? We put on Christ. The word Paul uses is endyō, which carries the meaning to clothe, endue, or have (put) on.[42] What a wonderful reminder as we get up each morning. Just as we wouldn't leave the house without trading our jammies for work clothes, we shouldn't begin any work without putting on Christ. This looks like a daily habit of sitting quietly before the Lord, and inviting Him to transform our hearts and lives. It is intentionality; it requires a posture of humility and an acknowledgment of dependence. It requires a mindset shift—a realization that the God of the Universe not only provided a way for us to be forgiven for our sins,[43] but also intercedes for us *today.*[44] When we recognize this truth, and respond with action, our lives change. We are able to live not as victims of our circumstances, but as transformed Christ-followers, learning to reflect His image and power. This is real power. This is the same power that Paul reminded Timothy to put on.

We aren't meant to mother on empty, but rather in the faith and love, which are in Christ Jesus.

Mom on Guard

Guard, through the Holy Spirit who dwells in us,
the treasure which has been entrusted to you.

2 TIMOTHY 1:14

First-time parents understand the need for being vigilant. From the moment their tiny, fragile human comes home from the hospital, they watch their chest for rhythmic breathing at night. They check their fontanels for signs of dehydration. When the child starts to gain mobility, they baby-proof all the electrical outlets, and put away all choking hazards. Parents do this because they know the safety of their child is at stake, and ultimately, they are responsible to keep their little one from injury.

New parents are most likely maintaining a rigid schedule to promote good sleep hygiene and proper mental development. Often this same zeal for order has waned by the second child, and by the third or fourth, it is easy to fall into an almost comfortable rhythm of treading water. This isn't necessarily a problem. At times, it is simply a necessity. However, as parents, we can never lose our vigilance for the needs and well-being of our children. This is, after all, our job.

In his letter to Timothy, Paul called for a similar skill set. He told his protégé to "guard" or "to keep watch"[45] over the treasure entrusted to him. This is almost a direct echo of Paul's closing remarks to Timothy in his previous epistle where he exhorted him, "O Timothy, guard what has been entrusted to you, avoiding worldly and empty chatter" (1 Timothy 6:20a). Paul's thoughts in his last days were consumed by the furthering of the Gospel and the purity of its this message. His encouragement reminded Timothy to remain true to his purpose and calling—that is to avoid anything that would sully his ability to share the Good News of Jesus.

As mothers, how do we faithfully do our part to mother the children God has given us and steward the treasure of God's Word in our home? These tasks happen simultaneously. They happen by knowing the Word, and by knowing our kids.

Unfortunately, there are no shortcuts to either task. You only know the Word by spending time in it. You only develop relationships with your children by spending time with them.

Application for this will look different for each family, but will require some common fundamental elements—like spending time with the Lord. For many people, this means getting up early, and taking time to read the Bible and pray. Maybe you stay up late. But time isn't the most important factor. Consistency is.

Your kids need eye contact and real, meaningful conversations. This can be difficult for busy working moms who have little free time, which makes those interactions all the more meaningful. Take time to talk to your children. Sit on the ground and play tea party, ask them how their day was, and stay mentally present to hear their response. Just listen—no checking your grocery list, paying your mortgage, or scrolling social media. Your children know when they have your full attention.

For stay-at-home moms, this also requires intentionality. Take time to do things your children enjoy in order to build those bonds and develop the relationship that they desperately need. Maybe your kids love video games, but the loud electronic noises drive you nuts. Play every now and then. Bake cookies with your kids, taking pleasure in the opportunity of making them feel included and needed. Growing your lives together is a meaningful and necessary part of parenting.

But just parenting isn't enough. It is in the best interest of our children to be capable teachers of God's Word so they will have sound instruction to adhere to. We complete the Great Commission in our corner of the earth, evangelizing and discipling whoever God puts in our path. We guard the treasure of God's Word so that future generations know the Good News of Jesus. Only by God's grace, we mother with competence.

Mama, how are you doing at faithfully raising the children in your home and treasuring the Word of God? Explain:

_____

_____

_____

_____

_____

_____

_____

_____

_____

EIGHT

MOTHERING WITH GRACE

You are aware of the fact that all who are in Asia turned away from me, among whom are Phygelus and Hermogenes. The Lord grant mercy to the house of Onesiphorus, for he often refreshed me and was not ashamed of my chains; but when he was in Rome, he eagerly searched for me and found me—the Lord grant to him to find mercy from the Lord on that day—and you know very well what services he rendered at Ephesus.

2 TIMOTHY 1:15-18

THERE ARE MANY BENEFITS to living in a small town. Where we live, one iconic iron bridge neatly bisects the town. This bridge is the only source of traffic jams, which seldom amount to more than four or five cars waiting for the light to change. At the post office, the workers know which box is yours, and will even deliver your packages to your car if you have too many packages and too few hands. Small towns have shop clerks who know your name, trucks that honk with recognition as you put out the trash, and strangers—who knows someone who knows you--text you to let you know you left your gate open.

Small towns also include people who air their dirty laundry in group threads, at church, with other moms at the local co-op. And, since everyone knows everyone, all tidbits of gossip are normally relevant and interesting to everyone. In such tight-knit communities, it helps to keep your laundry list short simply because the person you're complaining about is probably the mother, or cousin, or sister of the person you're grousing to.

In 2 Timothy 1:15, Paul recounts to Timothy the sad truth of how his loss of freedom had caused him to be totally deserted by fellow believers. He mentions two believers by name, Phygelus and Hermogenes, whom nothing else is known.

Charles Spurgeon writes, "Probably these were leaders who ought to have acted differently and to have stuck by the apostle. But, when he was in prison, and likely to be put to death by Nero, many who had been his former companions forsook him and were ashamed to own him."[46]

Paul also mentions that "all who were in Asia turned away from me." Men and women who Paul had ministered with had abandoned him in his moment of greatest need. These were believers he was talking about. People who should have known better, but didn't act better. In a way, Paul's abandonment mirrored Christ's desertion at His arrest and trial,[47] yet His response to this ill-treatment was very different.

When Christ was denied by Peter, He initiated restoring the relationship shortly after His resurrection.[48] Paul's relationship with Phygelus and Hermogenes appears irrevocably severed. Perhaps the apostle harbored bitterness against these men, or maybe he simply lacked the opportunity to reestablish relationship with them in his incarcerated state. Perhaps his heart mourned this deep betrayal, but he did so with complete forgiveness. Scripture doesn't comment on this. However, the same apostle, inspired by the Holy Spirit, also wrote in his letter to the Roman church, "Never pay back evil for evil to anyone. Respect what is right in the sight of all men. If possible, so far as it depends on you, be at peace with all men" (Romans 12:17-18).

So how do we reconcile the betrayal of someone close to us? Was Paul sinning by openly telling Timothy about these men who had wronged him? Was he merely warning his colleague to avoid close partnership with them himself? We don't know. However, Scripture does delineate guidelines for how a believer should navigate difficult interpersonal relationship issues.

In the Book of Ephesians, Paul exhorts believers by saying, "Let no unwholesome word proceed from your mouth, but only such *a word* as is good for edification according to the need *of the moment*, so that it will give grace to those who hear" (Ephesians 4:29). And just two verses later, he gives the exhortation, "Let all bitterness and wrath and anger and clamor and slander be put away from you, along with all malice" (Ephesians 4:31). Christians are to be characterized by holiness in their speech. Our words are to be chosen with purpose and precision, to build up those around us.

What a joy for those whose words and testimony are harmonized. Living in a small town is a powerful reminder for the need to be free from verbal duplicity. In a tight-knit community, you can't escape what you say. So when believers have speech that is "always...with grace, as though seasoned with salt,"[49] there is nothing to escape from. A short laundry list is crucial to maintaining a godly testimony before an onlooking world.

Authentic Encouragement

The Lord grant mercy to the house of Onesiphorus,
for he often refreshed me and was not ashamed
of my chains. But when he was in Rome, he
eagerly searched for me and found me.

2 TIMOTHY 1:16-17

How many of us can remember small acts of kindness shown to us? For me, this list includes a time during my college years when a middle-aged woman from my church took me in and fed me—chicken and noodles on mashed potatoes. It was after the service on a Sunday, and at the time, this simple gesture meant so much more than the actual meal. It was friendship, kindness, and a sense of belonging. Around the same time, a dear friend of my dad's gave me a ride to a dreaded doctor's appointment, then encouraged me when I was frustrated with the results. Although his own body was riddled with cancer, he was focused on supporting me, pointing me to Christ in my own much smaller battle.

These were selfless acts of kindness, and motivated by hearts set solely on Christ and serving Him. Both deserved recognition for their generosity and humility. But how on earth did they do it? How much more often is true encouragement traded for its cheap substitute of superficial flattery and faux support?

Paul alluded twice in his writings to the dangers of flattery, writing in his letter to the Thessalonians, "For we never came with flattering speech, as you know, nor with a pretext for greed—God is witness," (1 Thessalonians 2:5) and again in his letter to the Roman Church:

> "Now I urge you, brethren, keep your eye on those who cause dissensions and hinderances contrary to the teaching which you have learned, and turn away from them. For such men are slaves, not of our Lord Christ but of their own appetites; and by their smooth and flattering speech they deceive the hearts of the unsuspecting" (Romans 16:17-18).

In the first verse, Paul uses a Greek word for flattery called kolakeia.[50] The latter verse uses a similar word, eulogia, which can mean "language artfully adapted to captivate the hearer."[51] In either case, the implications are clear. Flattery is prerequisite to manipulation, a temptation that Paul did his best to avoid.

It appears Paul never wasted time with cheap flattery. Scripture doesn't record him praising the external beauty or possessions of any of his friends. Instead, he commended men and women of the faith for their moral character and spiritual edification. In the Book of Romans, Paul recognized Phoebe for her many acts of service.[52] He also highlights the tremendous risks that Prisca and Aquila had taken for the benefit of the Gentile church.[53] He encouraged believers in the faith by pointing out the working of the Holy Spirit in their lives. This was purposeful and productive, living out the God's mandate: "Therefore encourage one another and build up one another, just as you also are doing" (1 Thessalonians 5:11).

In this same pattern of encouragement, Paul shared the testimony of Onesiphorous, who ministered to the apostle when he needed the reassurance so deeply. It seems the man lived in Ephesus, as evidenced by Paul sending greetings by way of Timothy.[54] Yet, when he was in Rome, he searched out and ministered to the incarcerated apostle. What a welcomed relief this kind brother's presence must have been, especially as Roman prisoners often depended on friends or family to supply their most basic of needs. Onesiphorous was willing to assume "guilt by association" and brave the most horrifying of conditions to minister to this suffering saint. What courage he showed. What dependence upon the Holy Spirit. What selflessness. These were traits worth sharing about, and so Paul did. He not only offered his testimony as a means of gratitude, but also of inspiration—the work of the Holy Spirit.

Seldom do women, even Christian women, strive to build each other up with such meaningful words. How often do we settle for surface-level complements rather than reaching one another at a deeper soul-level? But this is what we need; to be generous with genuine reinforcement, sharing the good we see in our brothers and sisters and *kids!*

Is your son controlling his anger and exhibiting a gentle spirit? Celebrate that Jesus is changing him. Is your daughter learning to submit to your guidelines for dress? Praise her for her growth in humility. Don't settle for the flattery the world is dishing out. Seek to encourage those around you in the way that will point them to Jesus.

Blessed to Be a Blessing

The Lord grant to him to find mercy from the
Lord on that day—and you know very well
what services he rendered at Ephesus.

2 TIMOTHY 1:18

Motherhood starts right off with a great opportunity to learn what it means to be a blessing. We spend the first nine months of our child's life in the giving of our body for their very existence. We get ill, we gain weight, we ache in places that never hurt before. We birth our tiny children with no small amount of pain, and immediately set to the task of feeding them and tending to their needs around the clock. We shower only after they are soothed and settled. We feed them at the expense of our sleep and our convenience. And yet, what a blessed calling.

Motherhood is replete with many different seasons, some more difficult than others. The season in which my third child was born, we moved four times in three months. It was hard! Morning sickness with my fourth was hard. But these situations likely pale to the difficulties that some of you mamas have waded through or continue to wade through. Perhaps your season of motherhood is tough. But whatever difficulty God has called you to, He has given you an opportunity to be a blessing in the midst of it. We see this modeled so beautifully in the letter of 2 Timothy.

Remember Paul's circumstances, from a position of physical deprivation, pain, isolation and loneliness, he sought the wellbeing of Onesiphorous, asking for the Lord's eternal blessing on him. In essence, he longed that one day the Lord would say of this faithful brother, "Well done, good and faithful slave...enter into the joy of your master" (Matthew 25:23). He mentions twice a desire for the Lord to show mercy to Onesiphorous, both to his household and at the final Judgement.

What a powerful reminder this was for a condemned man to pray. And yet, with his eyes ever focused on Christ, Paul understood that his future was certain. With confidence he was able to say that, "The Lord will rescue me from every evil deed, and will bring me safely to His heavenly kingdom; to Him *be* the glory forever and ever. Amen" (2 Timothy 4:18). Paul was able to minister to others with a grateful heart, even from a place of suffering.

Bringing it Home

Paul was deeply wounded by the desertion of his co-laborers Phygelus and Hermogenes. Perhaps these men still followed Christ, but they just weren't willing to associate with the incarcerated apostle. The simple kindness of caring shown by Onesiphorous was so life-giving, it was remembered and blessed by Paul, and immortalized in the pages of Scripture. What strong contrasting responses to a hurting man.

How do these principles of mothering with grace play out in the mundane of our lives? We mother with grace when we tend to the needs of those God has placed around us. Perhaps we are the Onesiphorous God has called to minister to an aging relative dealing with memory loss. If so, we can do it for the glory of God,[55] realizing our service, no matter how menial or discouraging, is of eternal value. Maybe our lives have been deeply scarred by adult children or a spouse that has deserted us. We press on in grace, learning to rely more heavily on the strength and love of Jesus Christ.

Maybe we need grace for the relentless needs of several

small children who seem oblivious to our hard work and our feelings. In these times, we mother with grace by serving them without sarcasm or traces of martyrdom. We offer our actions as a sacrifice to the Lord, rather than to the tiny humans who share our DNA. Finally, we go about our day as an act of worship.

Motherhood is a reminder that God has called us to a life where we rely on Him and His grace. When our flesh begs for gratification in the form of gossip or complaining, we are struck afresh with the grace that God has given us—a way for our own sinful hearts to be forgiven. The practical applications for this truth are endless, but the principle is the same. Within the four walls that we call home, we can extend this same grace to our own families, as unto Christ.

Who has blessed you and helped you in your mothering journey? Have you taken the time to tell them?

_____

_____

_____

_____

_____

NINE

BE STRONG

You therefore, my son, be strong in
the grace that is in Christ Jesus.

2 TIMOTHY 2:1

BE STRONG, MAMA! THIS seemingly positive mantra has been peddled and repackaged by feminists, fitness instructors, and a host of motivational speakers since the dawn of marketing. Susan B. Anthony encouraged this basic tenant when advocating for Women's Suffrage. The iconic Rosie the Riveter appealed to this sense of woman-power when women's presence in the workforce was needed in World War II. Yes, power sells! As women, we subscribe to the affirmation, "Anything you can do, I can do better." And this includes child-rearing—while juggling a home, our age and hormones, with limited time and depleted energy, because we like to believe we have access to a 36-hour day.

While these are culturally popular ideas, God's concept of a strong woman differs greatly from what is advertised on TV. We love the verses in Scripture like "I can do all things through Him who strengthens me" (Philippians 4:13) as well as the popular introduction to the armor of God, "Finally, be strong in the Lord and in the strength of His might" (Ephesians 6:10). These verses, along with the one at the beginning of the chapter, are remarkably Instagram-worthy because they feel *so good*. They sound like God wants to make us into the tough, overachieving, fit and fantastic mothers we all desire to be. Yet, context is key.

The original word employed by Paul in each of these verses is endynamoō, which means "to receive strength, be strengthened or increase in strength" and also to "be bold, headstrong."[56] This definition directs our focus to the original recipient of Paul's epistle, Timothy. The young pastor about to be separated from his spiritual mentor and deep friend, lived in a world where Christians were hated, hunted down, and killed. Paul had just mentioned that he had faced the desertion of two of his companions. Likely, he expected a similar fate for Timothy as he used the following verses to remind him to be willing to suffer for Jesus.

With this final letter, Paul repeated to Timothy how he needed not only to be strong, but to be strong in the grace *that is in Christ Jesus*. The task that Timothy was left with—teaching his flock and leading a new generation of Christ-followers—was daunting, to say the least. Scripture records that he was imprisoned at least once,[57] and, as Church tradition accounts, Timothy died a martyr's death about 30 years after Paul. Timothy had need to be strong. Only by relying on the grace of Jesus would Timothy have had the strength to complete his ministry.

What does this type of strength look like in our lives? In the Book of Ephesians, we see the same word for strength employed in the description of the armor of God. In this passage, Paul exhorts believers to be strong in the Lord and in His strength to put on the armor of God in order to withstand the attacks of the devil. Paul uses the Greek word endyō, which reflects the idea of actively dressing for battle, much like a trained soldier would do.[58] This active verb tense is intentional; we do not happen to be prepared to engage in spiritual warfare. We are not accidentally strong Christians. We are strong in the Lord through a daily decision to follow Him, and to avail ourselves of the spiritual resources Christ has made possible.

We live in a time that is equally dark. Perhaps more than ever before, our children need mamas who are dressed for battle, girded about with truth in a world that says truth is subjective. We should be clothed in righteousness, consciously separated from the world in the things that are overtly evil. Our every footstep should be directed and bathed in the Good News of the Gospel, which we have prepared and rehearsed so we are ready to share it with those who need to hear.

With God's Word in our hearts, He is active in our minds so we can counter the claims of the world with dexterity and wisdom. Being strong in the grace that is in Christ Jesus doesn't simply mean that we shoot up a quick bullet prayer, asking that we don't snap at a whiny child. Rather, it evokes an image that we are not only filled with strength *by* Jesus Christ, but also *for* Him so that we are equipped with what we need to be capable warriors in a world that has turned so far from Him.

Be Strong in Mind

Somewhere along the development of memes, childhood became open season for cheap comedy. There are comedic moments to raising kids, for sure. Like when my children dress up in the clothes of mine and my husband, and walked around the house all evening imitating us. They were armed to the teeth with oversized shoes, a spatula, and a heaping helping of "no!" We have all laughed over the funny things our little ones have said as they were discovering the world. We stifle guffaws as our toddlers mimic our actions with great bravado. However, the sheer volume of videos dedicated to obstinate toddlers and clueless parents suggest that we live in a time where parents are simply not strong minded.

In the Book of Proverbs, parents are commanded to "Train up a child in the way he should go, even when he is old he will not depart from it."[59] The concept of "train up" is to initiate or discipline; also to dedicate.[60] It is hardly a term of passivity, but rather of purposeful planning and dedicated follow-through. We are to be strong in the way that we mother, convicted in the choices we make, and disciplined to bring them to completion. We see this same type of tenacious dedication to the home and family illustrated in Proverbs 31 and its woman of virtue. King Solomon outlines several relevant qualities of this godly woman in verses 15 through 30:

She is diligent, preparing the food her family needs.

She is wise with her money and invests in things that are profitable.

She is attentive to her physical needs, rather than lazy.

She is confident in the value of her work.

She prepares for the needs of her family before the need arrives.

She speaks wisely and kindly.

She fears the Lord.

Although this list is hardly exhaustive, we get a general picture of what God is expecting of us. This woman is characterized by diligence, discipline, and follow-through in every area of her life. Her entire world is shaped by her fear of the Lord. The result is that the things she does are profitable and stand up to the test of time. God needs mothers like this, who see their calling to motherhood as an all-encompassing task, and who implement thoughtful, prayerful methods for child-rearing. God wants mothers who are wise with their words and their money, who steward their resources well, and do not fall into passivity. Mothers who take care of their own physical needs, not out of vanity, but a desire to steward well the body God has given them.

And yet, somewhere along the way, decisive, thoughtful mothering has fallen out of vogue and been replaced with wishy-washy women listening to countless podcasts in an endless quest to figure out how to "do life." And so many mamas contemplate whether they should co-sleep, breastfeed, homeschool, or send their children to trade school depending on the opinion of perfect strangers.

These are all important decisions—truly. Yet, the raising of our children should avoid becoming a byproduct of whatever flavor popular culture is peddling to the parent. For these weighty decisions and countless others, it's sad to think that we could become "fair weather" mamas. If you choose to homeschool, you should know why. Is it because your friends do? *Not such a good reason.* Is it because you've heard from God that this is His purpose for your life? Then push forward with a plan in mind, and also yield to the direction of the Lord.

This applies to all seasons of motherhood, those learning to be empty-nesters as well as grandparents. It's important to continue in a pattern of faithfully seeking the Lord, and sticking to a plan when moving forward according to His will. When welcoming foster children or adopted children into your family, humbly seek God's best plan for your lives, and your little ones. As King Solomon shares in Proverbs, "In all your ways acknowledge Him, and He will make your paths straight" (Proverbs 3:6).

We can only mother with a strong mind when we are actively seeking the Lord and His will. We know His will when we take the time to dwell in His presence and learn from His Word. We can move forward in confidence when we take the time to thoughtfully consider a course of action, pray over it with a spouse or trusted godly counselor, and weigh out all the implications of that choice. When we are sure that we are acting in the best interest of our little ones and in accordance with God's Word, then we can step out—purposefully, confidently. This applies to medications and vaccinations and school choice. It encompasses cell phone usage, and when we allow our children to date. These are decisions that the Lord does care about. All we need do is to seek His will, and then move forward undeterred regarding what the rest of the world thinks.

Strong in Conviction

Conviction is an indomitable force. In an age that deems absolutes repugnant, understanding the truth of the Gospel—what it is and what it is not—is crucial.

Because there are those who will always question, Paul's command to Timothy to be strong is no less relevant today. There are countless doubters, innumerable scoffers. Those who hurl every criticism at the most basic tenants of our faith through carefully constructed arguments. The question is, do we know how to respond? Do our children?

Maybe you grew up in the church, and have lived life

surrounded by a community of believers. Maybe your Bible is highlighted in a nacreous array of yellow, green, and pink markers, and you have Scripture art in every room of the house. A culture of Christianity is an awesome gift. But familiarity can breed apathy, the sort that keeps us from knowing God's Word enough to defend it when challenged.

Maybe you are a baby Christian, unsure where to start with your newfound faith. You understand the Gospel message, but don't feel confident in wading through theology that might sound pretty good, but you're not quite sure why.

Perhaps you know the Bible well. You have your cross-references all cross-referenced, and your concordance right next to your cup of coffee every morning. Maybe you faithfully study the Word and are more than able to sniff out ideas that are teetering on the edge of heresy, or perhaps have completely fallen off the bandwagon. The good news is, that no matter where you are in the spiritual growth continuum, your mandate is the same: "You therefore, my son, be strong in the grace that is in Christ Jesus."[61]

We are called to grow in strength, and to lead our children in the truth.

So where do we start? We become rock-solid on what the Gospel means to be "saved," and can articulate that truth. What is the Gospel? Perhaps the most succinct passage that explains it is found in 1 Corinthians 15:3-4:

> "For I delivered to you as of first importance what I also received, that Christ died for our sins according to the Scriptures, and that He was buried, and that He was raised on the third day according to the Scriptures."

The Gospel is God's grace to sinners, that we can be made right with Him. God is clear about the exclusivity of the Gospel,[62] and the necessity of the Holy Spirit to illumine our hearts so we can grasp its message.[63] And it is our job to be students of the Word so we know these truths deeper than a simple chapter-and-verse sort of familiarity. As Christians, these verses are core to the fiber of our being. We willingly entrust our eternal future to the veracity of these claims.

In addition to knowing the Gospel, we should absolutely have Scripture committed to memory, just as familiar as the faces of our children and the world that they live in. We can't assume that our kiddos are safe from spiritual attack because they go to a certain school, have amiable friends, or wear or don't wear specific clothes. If they have access to the internet (or have friends or siblings that do) they are open to countless attacks against their faith and their identity. It is our job to actively respond to these threats.

Why We Aren't Strong

In his classic Christian fiction work, *Screwtape Letters*, C.S. Lewis shared the correspondence of two demons attempting to shipwreck a believer in his faith. One of the tactics he suggested as salient was the anesthetic of pleasure and distraction:

> "And Nothing is very strong: strong enough to steal away a man's best years not in sweet sins but in a dreary flickering of the mind over it knows not what and knows not why, in the gratification of curiosities so feeble that the man is only half aware of them, in drumming of fingers and kicking of heels, in whistling tunes

that he does not like, or in the long, dim labyrinth of reveries that have not even lust or ambition to give them a relish, but which, once chance association has started them, the creature is too weak and fuddled to shake off."

If we aren't strong, it's because we are distracted.

Mamas, we live in a time replete with distractions. One recent study shared that Americans check their cell phones 144 times per day, totaling about 4 hours and 25 minutes spent on their device each day.[64] How are we supposed to have disciplined minds when our train of thought is perpetually jolted about like a pinball machine? We are surrounded by the numbing din of information. We have endless entertainment at our fingertips, and are never truly challenged intellectually. Our waning strength may also be due to the distractions of sin or because we are unlearned in our faith, or we are unmotivated to grow.

We also live in a time where our children desperately need us to be engaged and strong in our convictions—in other words, strong minded. They require solid, resilient mamas who are ready to stand up for the truth, for their sake as well as the sake of their children.

Are you up for the challenge to be that woman?

How can you implement tangible ways to be a strong and focused mother?

TEN

PRACTICE AND REPEAT

*The things which you have heard from me in the
presence of many witnesses, entrust these to faithful
men who will be able to teach others also.*

2 TIMOTHY 2:2

MANY OF THE ANCIENT civilizations have been shaped by a rich legacy of oral tradition. In cultures that do not have a written alphabet, the transmission of their language is dependent upon firsthand accounts. In an age where social interaction depends so heavily upon our technology, this concept seems archaic. However, oral tradition plays an important role in the strengthening of family ties and ingrafting a sense of community.

Think about the stories that are told over family get-togethers. Perhaps your family revisits memories of an excited younger sibling on Christmas morning or reminisce about family trips to Grandma's house over summer vacations. These shared recollections, ingrained in your mind through repetition, are a powerful bonding agent. No matter how hard social media or other electronic mediums try to replace it, nothing can usurp the power of a well-told story.

But sometimes, simply recounting a story isn't going to be good enough. There must be accuracy in the message. Have you ever asked a two-year-old to relay a message? You might have a frantic older child come bursting into the house screaming, *"She said there was a snake in the toilet"* or *"He said he'd put the keys away."* Reliability of a source matters.

As Paul was tying up the finished business of his ministry, he wanted to ensure that recounting of the Gospel was not going to be haphazardly shared. So, with painstaking clarity, he reminded Timothy to share the Word precisely, in a way it could be proliferated for generations to come.

What was the message that Timothy had received from Paul? The Gospel, clearly. But also extensive training in Christlikeness and discipleship through serving alongside him.[65] Timothy's name is mentioned in multiple apostolic greetings,[66] and he was the recipient of two epistles. Timothy was made privy to much of the New Testament as it was being written. He was an eyewitness of the transformational power of the Gospel as seen in the building of the Christian Church. Paul was reminding him of the truth of Scripture, that "From everyone who has been given much, much will be required; and to whom they entrusted much, of him they will ask all the more" (Luke 12:48b). Timothy had been given a rich spiritual heritage through his mother and grandmother, and incredible discipling as he served alongside Paul. Now he was challenged to put that investment to use.

Who Could Forget?

It seems incredible that the Apostle Paul went to such great lengths to encourage Timothy to keep the message of the Gospel pure and unsullied. After all, it had been less than 60 years since the Lord Jesus had lived on the earth. Many people who had been touched by Him, healed by Him, still existed on this side of the grave. The scribes and Pharisees still shuddered at the stories circulated about a man who had claimed to be the Messiah, and whose miraculous disappearance could not be explained. Surely children present at the feeding of the 5,000 had told their children the miracles of Jesus. Certainly those witnesses at the Cross who saw the graves open and the temple curtain torn in two had not all died yet. If there were still witnesses alive, why would a prominent leader in the church feel the need to employ such strong, repetitive reminders to adhere to the truth of the Gospel. Who could forget?

But, as any mama can tell you, we forget. We forget when certain children hit developmental milestones. We forget birthdays and other important events. Worst of all, sometimes we forget about Jesus. It is easy to get busy with the doing of life—so busy that we forget that we have a risen Savior, the One who is fully God and fully man, who gave His life and rose again so we could be forgiven for our sins.

We try to white-knuckle our way through a parenting problem or a season of difficulty on the strength of our organizational skills, networking skills, or work ethic, rather than humbly accepting the strength that God freely offers to those who will receive Christ. We all do this.

We, who have the Holy Spirit living inside of us.

We, who have the full cannon of Scripture within easy reach.

We, who have a plethora of platforms for teaching and accountability.

We forget from the comfort of our homes.

We simply forget because we're human.

How much easier would it be for us to distort or dismiss the truth of the Gospel if it cost us our lives or the lives of our children? This was the reality of life in the time that Timothy lived and taught. People who followed Christ paid for it with their lives. Therefore, the Gospel needed to be shared out of obedience to Christ, and also for those who died in vain.

The stakes were high. They still are.

Throughout the history of Israel, the people forgot God. From the time the nation was liberated from slavery to Egypt, God called them to establish Passover so as to remember God's intervention on their behalf. And yet, the Book of 2 Kings shares that this religious celebration had not been practiced for the majority of Israel's time as a free people:

> "Then the king commanded all the people saying, 'Celebrate the Passover to the Lord your God as it is written in this book of the covenant.' Truly such a Passover had not been celebrated from the days of the judges who judged Israel, nor in all the days of the kings of Israel and of the kings of Judah. But in the eighteenth year of King Josiah, this Passover was observed to the Lord in Jerusalem" 2 Kings 23:21-23.

The people forgot or they deliberately chose not to obey. Whatever the reason, they disobeyed the direct command to remember God and to establish rhythms of remembrance in their culture to commemorate His faithfulness. The book of Judges is replete with examples of this pattern repeated. The people forgot God. Their spiritual negligence resulted in tragic loss and military oppression. Hence the Judges were established—whose job was to bring back the people into a right relationship with God.[67]

When the Nation of Israel demanded a physical king, God understood this was a further rejection of His power and authority over them.[68] And yet, He allowed a monarchy to replace His theocracy, as His people turned their back on Him with obscene boldness. The major prophets warned of judgement if they continued in their sins.[69] The minor prophets offered hope for those who would repent.[70] And when Jesus came, the apostle John writes, "He was in the world, and the world was made through Him, and the world did not know Him. He came to His own, and those who were His own did not receive Him" (John 1:10-11).

God's chosen people forgot Him again and again. This should give us immense hope because God continued to pursue them, even when they were not faithful. Paul understood Scripture. He knew human nature and how weak people can be. Yet again, he reminded Timothy that the message of the Gospel was worth telling—over and over. The church must not forget.

A Winsome Witness

The things which you have heard from me in the presence of many witnesses, entrust these to faithful men who will be able to teach others also.

2 TIMOTHY 2:2

December 7, 1941, was a crucial moment in American history. With the surprise attack of Japanese forces on Pearl Harbor, Hawaii, the United States Pacific Fleet was decimated. More than 2,400 Americans lost their lives in the onslaught that day, and 1,000 more were injured. This attack served as the impetus for America declaring war on Japan and officially entering World War II.

While the attack was a surprise, tensions between the countries had been present for decades, and conflict seemed inevitable. The true tragedy of Pearl Harbor was that Japan declared war on the United States prior to the attack; however, the message was not decrypted in time. The warning had been given, but the message wasn't shared. History cannot predict what might have happened if America could have prepared for the attack that Sunday morning. But we are left to wonder if the heavy casualties could have been avoided.

A witness has a crucial job; they are to pass information from source to source. In the case of Pearl Harbor, the cryptographer was entrusted with a message that directly impacted the lives of thousands of Americans. In 2 Timothy, Paul reminded Timothy of his need to pass along the message, both of the Good News of the Gospel, but also the teachings that he had received at the hands of his spiritual mentor. Like the attack on Pearl Harbor, this message required urgency and precision in the sharing of a live-saving truth. Timothy was responsible to disciple and prepare those who were competent to share the teachings of Christ with future generations.

Many mission organizations today recycle this model of reproducibility—a key concept for the possibility of church growth. Timothy wasn't merely responsible to train his own congregation. It wasn't enough for his church to have the right programs and ministry opportunities. He was to train disciples who would then train other disciples. We are to follow this example; to practice obedience to Christ's Great Commission.

"Go therefore and make disciples of all the nations, baptizing them in the name of the Father and the Son and the Holy Spirit, 20 teaching them to observe all that I commanded you" (Matthew 28:19-20a).

This discipling starts within our own homes—as we make breakfast, drive to co-op, and help with science fair projects. We make disciples of our children as we teach them the Word in the everyday moments of our lives. But that's not where it ends. We are mandated to make disciples of all the nations. As Paul so wisely puts in his letter to the Romans, "How then will they call on Him in whom they have not believed? How will they believe in Him whom they have not heard? And how will they hear without a preacher?" (Romans 10:14).

This means us! Mamas, we have a unique opportunity to pour into the lives of our children by nurturing their hearts as they grow and develop. We have the responsibility to point them to Jesus, and to train them in His ways. But what about the mom you chat with at ballet class? What about the teenage kid who delivers your curbside orders? We are commanded to make disciples of *all* nations. That means *everyone*.

The message is just as urgent today as it was 2,000 years ago. What a privilege we've been given to spread God's message of mercy and forgiveness!

Christ's Self-Sustaining Church

Then the seventh angel sounded; and there were loud voices in heaven, saying, "The kingdom of the world has become the kingdom of our Lord and of His Christ; and He will reign forever and ever." And

*the twenty-four elders, who sit on their thrones
before God, fell on their faces and worshiped God.*

REVELATION 11:15-16

In the end, Christ's Kingdom will be built. Jesus Christ is coming back, and the need for faithful witnesses will be obsolete. People will *see* the risen Christ, glorified and all-powerful. He will rule and reign all people, and every knee will bow to Him and confess Him as Lord.[71] Jesus does not need us in order to rule and reign on earth and Heaven. He will rule. He will reign. The only question is will we be obedient right now to what He asks us to do?

This confidence in Christ building His church sustained Paul in prison awaiting his execution. He was not anxious that Timothy would fail and that Christianity would be snuffed out. He had hope in the power of the Gospel, and in the power of Jesus Christ to complete God's good plan. He simply wanted to see His friend serve well.

There is so much peace in a mindset like Paul's. We too can be settled in the truth that Christ will build His church. He will rule. He will reign. As it says in the book of Daniel,

> "For His dominion is an everlasting dominion,
> and His kingdom endures from generation to
> generation. All the inhabitants of the earth are
> accounted as nothing, But He does according to
> His will in the host of heaven" (Daniel 4:35).

Mamas, this is a message we are commanded to repeat. This is a message worth repeating.

What everyday discipleship could you implement into your home?

_____

_____

_____

_____

_____

_____

ELEVEN

A LIFE DEDICATED

Suffer hardship with me, as a good soldier of Christ Jesus. No soldier in active service entangles himself in the affairs of everyday life, so that he may please the one who enlisted him as a soldier. Also if anyone competes as an athlete, he does not win the prize unless he competes according to the rules. The hard-working farmer ought to be the first to receive his share of the crops. Consider what I say, for the Lord will give you understanding in everything.

2 TIMOTHY 2:3-7

EVANGELIST BILLY GRAHAM FAMOUSLY said; "It is true that salvation is free, but discipleship costs everything." He went on to say, "It is true that very few of us would volunteer to endure physical suffering, but this is precisely what Jesus promises. And He asks it of us. He asks that we commit ourselves to Him without reservation and that we be willing to pay whatever price it takes to follow Him."[72]

Discipleship requires self-denial. Jesus said it outright to His followers while on earth; "If anyone wishes to come after Me, he must deny himself, and take up his cross daily and follow Me" (Luke 9:23b). The cross, an instrument of execution, has for millennia been the standard of the Christian faith. It is the means of salvation and symbolizes the rugged path to sanctification. This brand of dedication is uncomfortable in our post-Christian Western culture. We prefer our faith to be a part of us, rather than a Master to whom we owe everything. And yet, with three familiar images, Paul paints the picture of devoted service to Christ, service that requires everything of the believer.

The Mindset of Dedication

The Soldier. The Athlete. The Farmer. Three distinctly different vocations; different stations, each requiring unwavering commitment to the job. The Soldier would have been an all-too familiar image to many in Paul's day, as the massive reach of the Roman empire required guards roaming the streets to maintain order. These men were wholly dedicated to their assignments, and could be punished with death for failure. They were simultaneously an image of power and submission, living their lives obedient to their commanding officer.

As alluded to in this passage, soldiers were also called to live separate from their civilian counterparts. Theologian Charles Spurgeon explained it this way: "It was a law in Rome that no soldier was to plead in court for another as a bailiff... or to have to have anything to do, while a soldier, with either husbandry, or merchandise."[73]

Likewise, the Apostle Paul references another image familiar to a first-century believer. The Athlete was a man who underwent rigorous training to compete in the Olympics or the Isthmian Games. Olympic athletes today face some of the same training rigors. Hours of practice. Extensive personal coaching. Countless days of preparation culminating in a single moment. For these athletes, their athletic goal requires absolute dedication and immense discipline.

The third image, the Farmer, lacks the physical accolades of the athlete or the power status of the soldier. A farmer is, by nature, hard-working. The word employed by Paul in this passage, *kopiaō*, means "to labor with wearisome effort, to toil."[74] By necessity, the farmer's life is one of never-ending sweat and strain. In the winter, he must keep his animals fed, and provide adequate shelter. In the cold months, he plans, prunes, and prepares. In the warm months, he tills and weeds and sprays against the blights that would destroy his crop. And he prays. He prays for rain; he prays for sufficient chill hours. He prays for the crop to come to fruition. The farmer, like the athlete and the soldier, is married to his work. His land needs him; and he it. Of these three images, John MacArthur writes,

> "The soldier often has the excitement of battle, and the athlete the thrill of competing. But most of the farmer's working hours are tedious, humdrum, and unexciting. And unlike the teacher, the soldier, and the athlete, a farmer often works alone. He has no students to stimulate him, no fellow soldiers to fight with him, no teammates or crowd to cheer him."[75]

Christians today need the mindset of the farmer, the athlete, and the soldier. These are men and women with an all-or-nothing resolve. They are people who have committed their everything to their life work and forgotten all other paths. This is the lifestyle of a believer, and the picture that Paul was painting. Christ Himself said it best in His earthly ministry,

"No one, after putting his hand to the plow and looking back, is fit for the kingdom of God" (Luke 9:62).

The Lifestyle of Dedication

Dedication is indicative of priority. One former Olympian and seven-time national track and field champion, Alysia Montaño corroborated that narrative. Montaño had competed on the global stage multiple times when she wanted to begin having a family. Running was her passion, but she also wanted children and was determined not to sacrifice one for the other. So, after becoming pregnant, Montaño kept training, and competed in the 2014 Track and Field National Championships one month before giving birth.[76] She then went on to form a charity to help women pursue their athletic goals once a mother.

Even to the non-athlete, Montaño's persistence to compete so late into pregnancy is inspirational. Her indomitable spirit allowed her to reach a goal few women even considered possible. She did so because her desire to compete fueled her ability to achieve.

What is the driving force that *we* would sacrifice for?

For Paul, the Gospel laid claim to every area of his life. He saw his flesh as dead, his life as wholly tied to Christ. He wrote a similar sentiment in his letter to the Galatian church when he said, "I have been crucified with Christ; and it is no longer I who live, but Christ lives in me; and the life which I now live in the flesh I live by faith in the Son of God, who loved me and gave Himself up for me" (Galatians 2:20). This exhortation was more than idle speech. Paul was calling Timothy to join him in a life marked by complete devotion to Jesus.

Mamas, we would do well to dwell on this calling and take honest stock of our own lives. Does Jesus consume our priorities? Is He the theme of our dedication? In a world fascinated with so many things, our children need mothers who are characterized by unwavering and complete dedication to Jesus Christ. Our relationship with Christ should permeate the nature of our mothering, the method of our discipline, and the tone of our responses. His grace should impact our daily reactions to all that is extraordinary and routinely ordinary.

In our home at Christmastime, we often make cinnamon ornaments. The brown cut-out dough is not particularly pretty, but when you complete the required two-hour bake time, the woody, spiced aroma fills the entire house. These little decorations are a quiet reminder of what a lifestyle of dedication to Christ looks like. The tiny gingerbread men and candy canes don't have to *will* themselves to spread their perfume. It's just what they do. It's their nature. The Apostle Paul explains this concept in his letter to the Corinthian church when he writes, "For we are a fragrance of Christ to God among those who are being saved and among those who are perishing; [16] to the one an aroma from death to death, to the other an aroma from life to life. And who is adequate for these things?" (2 Corinthians 2:15-16).

A lifestyle of dedication requires a singular purpose—to prioritize Christ above all else. This doesn't mean to "devalue" others, but to simply prioritize them beneath Jesus. To have Christ permeate your life means He takes priority over your identity as a mother, as a member of the workforce, as a certain ethnicity, over everything. Your identity in Christ is your complete identity. All your other responsibilities are merely out-workings of your position in Christ.

The application of this truth can be wiggled into your everyday life. You aren't a stay-at-home mother because you have four children and can't afford daycare. You are a stay-at-home mother because you believe that God has called you to a lifestyle, which includes 24- hour-a day discipleship of your children. You don't work at an office because your degree is in marketing or law or finance. You do it because God has gifted you with special abilities, and you see your job as an opportunity to represent Him well in the workplace. This is a fundamental identity change, and one that necessitates you give every aspect of your work to Jesus.

And so, when your children are difficult, your job is stressful, or the members of your women's ministry ungrateful, take a breath and recognize that your work isn't for them at all, but is an act of obedience to your Savior. In your corner of the world, you are to be the very best soldier, athlete, farmer, *or mama* that God has called you to be.

The Reward of Dedication

Children understand waiting with expectation. Scarcely are the dishes cleared from the Thanksgiving feast when their little eyes turn to decorating a tree and counting down to the twenty-fifth of December. Some parents help their young children measure the time with little Advent calendars, building daily excitement as box by tiny box gets checked off. And then, the moment they have long waited for. Christmas morning bursts with all the anticipation their tiny bodies can hold as they rush to tear into the packages their parents have set out for them. When the moment arrives, they are more than ready to receive the reward for their long wait.

Like a parent showing their child the ever-rearing Christmas day, Paul reminds Timothy that not everything in the Christian life is dogged dedication. This is part of it, but there is the reward—the day that all Christians wait to receive. Paul himself in his closing of this epistle to Timothy, echoes his own anticipation of reward. "In the future there is laid up for me the crown of righteousness, which the Lord, the righteous Judge, will award to me on that day; and not only to me, but also to all who have loved His appearing" (2 Timothy 4:8).

Paul was confident that the Lord, the righteous Judge, would fairly reward the work done for Him and in His name. He encouraged Timothy with this truth, telling him to consider these things.

Likely the young preacher needed this encouragement. The tone of the letter, replete with exhortations for faithfulness, suggests that Timothy had been beaten down by the cost of dedication. He needed to remember the reward. Perhaps he was ashamed of Paul, embarrassed by his misfortune. He needed to remember that Paul wasn't incarcerated because somehow he had failed, but that Paul was serving Christ in anticipation of the future glory that would soon be revealed to him. Paul once said, "Do you not know that those who run in a race all run, but *only* one receives the prize? Run in such a way that you may win" (1 Corinthians 4:24).

Paul understood that he was winning. He wanted that same victorious life of dedication for Timothy as well.

This passage spans time, and also demands obedience of us. As we read the call to dedicated servitude, we should recognize that Christ's expectations of us are the same as the Apostle Paul and every other man and woman who has claimed the name of Christ-follower.

Following Christ may never place us in a jail cell or facing imminent execution, but we are called to be single-minded in our devotion to Christ, regardless of whatever else we are asked to do. Our love for Christ must command our day jobs and our family life, and everything must pale in comparison to our obedience to our Master. As we serve, and mother, we do so with joyful confidence, full of hope that our obedience is well worth it, and will be richly rewarded.

What small choice can you make today to live a life dedicated to Christ?

_____

_____

_____

_____

_____

_____

_____

TWELVE

WITH EYES ON CHRIST

*Remember Jesus Christ, risen from the
dead, descendant of David, according to my
gospel, for which I incarcerate hardship even
to imprisonment as a criminal; but the word
of God is not imprisoned. For this reason I
endure all things for the sake of those who are
chosen, so that they also may obtain the salvation
which is in Christ Jesus and with it eternal
glory. It is a trustworthy statement:*

*For if we died with Him, we will also live with Him;
If we endure, we will also reign with Him;
If we deny Him, He also will deny us;
If we are faithless, He remains faithful,
for He cannot deny Himself.*

2 TIMOTHY 2:8-13

SEE IN YOUR MIND'S eye and consider the Apostle Paul and Timothy, separated geographically, yet joined in the Spirit. Paul saw the discouragement of the young preacher. He knew how low his friend must have felt in a time of intense persecution. Paul likely feared Timothy would give up. When Paul was at his physical worst, he was offering all he had to support his apprentice in the faith.

These verses, and the ones surrounding them, were Paul's way of stretching out his hand from his Roman prison cell, to comfort the preacher in his work. He was calling Timothy to remember Christ, and to be strong and confident in the power of the resurrection and the God who could raise the dead.

"Remember Jesus Christ, risen from the dead, descendant of David, according to my gospel" (2 Timothy 2:8).

Let us never let the glorious truth of the Gospel stale in our hearts.

Paul called Timothy to remember Christ Jesus. The original word implies literally, *to be mindful of Jesus.* What a profound yet simple command. Paul pointed to the Founder of their faith, the Finisher of their faith, and reminded the preacher of the Source of their faith. Jesus Christ was (and is) risen from the dead, the One and only who had the power over death and holds the keys to death and Hell.[77] The Resurrection of Jesus Christ is the validation of our faith. Paul himself wrote in his letter to the Corinthians:

> "For if the dead are not raised, not even Christ has been raised; and if Christ has not been raised, your faith is worthless; you are still in your sins. Then those also who have fallen asleep in Christ have perished. If we have hoped in Christ in this life only, we are of all men most to be pitied. But now Christ has been raised from the dead, the first fruits of those who are asleep. For since by a man came death, by a man

also came the resurrection of the dead. For as in Adam all die, so also in Christ all will be made alive" (1 Corinthians 15:16-22).

This reminder was a call to revitalization. Paul pointed Timothy not to the Cross, but to the empty tomb. He reminded Timothy to hold on because the sufferings for Christ that they endured, were for a Savior who had conquered death and was alive. They served the Omnipotent one. He couldn't give up now.

Never Truly Shackled

Remember Jesus Christ, risen from the dead, descendant of David, according to my gospel, for which I suffer hardship even to imprisonment as a criminal; but the word of God is not imprisoned. For this reason I endure all things for the sake of those who are chosen, so that they also may obtain the salvation which is in Christ Jesus and with it eternal glory.

2 TIMOTHY 2:8-10

In the time of this writing, Paul was in a physically and emotionally difficult place. He had experienced great suffering before, as he outlined in his letter to the Corinthian church:

"Five times I received from the Jews thirty-nine lashes. Three times I was beaten with rods, once I was stoned, three times I was shipwrecked, a night and a day I have spent in the deep. I have been on frequent journeys,

in dangers from rivers, dangers from robbers,
dangers from my countrymen, dangers from
the Gentiles, dangers in the city, dangers in
the wilderness, dangers on the sea, dangers
among false brethren; I have been in labor
and hardship, through many sleepless nights,
in hunger and thirst, often without food, in cold
and exposure" (2 Corinthians 11:24-27).

When Paul wrote in his letter to the Galatians, "I bear
on my body the brand-marks of Jesus" (Galatians 6:17b), he
likely did not speak in metaphor. The apostle had physically
suffered in accordance to the words of Christ, "But beware
of men, for they will hand you over to the courts and scourge
you in their synagogues; and you will even be brought before
governors and kings for My sake, as a testimony to them and
to the Gentiles" (Matthew 10:17-18).

Upon trusting Christ, Paul had traded the fine clothing
and distinction of an accomplished Pharisee for the rough
hands and humble clothes of a tentmaker. As the years of
discipleship cost him much, his body was scarred and
weather-beaten. In prison, he was likely gaunt from poor
nutrition, and his skin, chafed and raw from the relentless
Roman shackles.

If anyone could speak authoritatively on suffering, it was
Paul. Yet, from his position of extreme physical difficulty, he
rejoiced in overwhelming victory of the Gospel, the transcen-
dence of the Word of God, and for the ever-advancing Kingdom of God, built on the lives of faithful believers like him.

Paul didn't brush past his circumstances, but he didn't
dwell on them either. He understood that his usefulness to the

Kingdom of God included his time sitting in prison, waiting a final verdict from a lunatic Emperor. He understood his death was imminent.[78] Yet, his final days reflect a distinct hope, showing he had come to peace with physical challenges many years prior. He wrote on this topic in his letter to the Galatian church, stating,

> "For to me, to live is Christ and to die is gain. But if I am to live on in the flesh, this will mean fruitful labor for me; and I do not know which to choose. But I am hard-pressed from both directions, having the desire to depart and be with Christ, for that is very much better" (Philippians 1:21-23).

Paul understood his fate wasn't at the whim of Nero. He wasn't a victim of the wrath of jealous Jews. He was sharing the Gospel wherever Christ put him. He accepted the difficulties as they came, and he was ever eager for the day he would be welcomed into the presence of his Savior.

And so, from this place of imprisonment, Paul could celebrate. He drew strength from reminding himself of the glorious truth of the Gospel, and the fact that Christ would continue His work without him. He might be shackled, but the Word of God never would be.

Because He is Worth It

There is a scene in Scripture that has fueled martyrs for millennia. It has become the battle cry of believers on every continent. It offers hope to churches in countries where the Christian faith is forbidden, and ministers to the heart of mothers longing to reach their unsaved children. It's found in the Book of Revelation, chapter 7, where Jesus gives us a snapshot of the future, and helps us see His conclusion for the great drama of human history. At the end of all things, this is what will be:

> "After these things I looked, and behold, a great multitude which no one could count, from every nation and *all* tribes and peoples and tongues, standing before the throne and before the Lamb, clothed in white robes, and palm branches *were* in their hands; [10] and they cry out with a loud voice, saying, 'Salvation to our God who sits on the throne, and to the Lamb'" (Revelation 7:9-10).

Can we grasp what this future will be like when it has become reality? Believers from every corner of the earth, freely worshipping God as He deserves. What glory! As believers in Christ, we understand that the supreme good we desire is that all people know and serve Christ. Paul understood this too. It is almost as if he had caught a glimpse of these things, and said them in 2 Timothy, "My trials don't matter. It will be over soon. I press on for those others, those not yet surrounding the throne of God. Timothy, press on for them, too."

Why does this perseverance in suffering matter? Paul addresses this as well. He calls upon what he labels a "trustworthy statement" supposed by many scholars to be a sort of early creed or hymn. In it he gives four "if we" statements, each backed by the character and authority of God.

> "For if we died with Him, we will also live with Him; If we endure, we will also reign with Him; If we deny Him, He also will deny us; If we are

WITH EYES ON CHRIST

faithless, He remains faithful, for He cannot deny Himself" (2 Timothy 2:11b-13).

These statements were each addressed in the earthly teaching ministry of Christ, and serve to illuminate the character and actions of believers in the greater context of the character and nature of God. Jesus was explicit about the high cost of following Him, stating that true discipleship required the believer must die to self, for; "He who does not take his cross and follow after Me is not worthy of Me. He who has found his life will lose it, and he who has lost his life for My sake will find it" (Matthew 10:38b-39).

"For if we died with Him, we will also live with Him," is the first "if we" statement that encompasses the promise for the believer in Christ. It is a ready trade of all earthly comfort we experience in this life for the eternal glory we anticipate in the next. As one martyred missionary by the name of Jim Elliot said, "He is no fool who gives what he cannot keep to gain that which he cannot lose."[79] This is an acceptance of the Scripture truth that we each have been crucified with Christ and [we] no longer live, but Christ lives in [us]" (Galatians 2:20b). The statement means we live with empty hands in this life, completely surrendered to God's plans for us, even unto death. "If we endure, we will also reign with him."

Anticipating his own death for the Lord, this phrase encompassed Paul's earthly hope. In the closing of the epistle, Paul mentions a "crown of righteousness, which the Lord, the righteous Judge, will award to me on that day" (2 Timothy 4:8b). In his letter to the Ephesians, Paul elaborates this promise:

"But God, being rich in mercy, because of His

great love with which He loved us, even when we
were dead in our transgressions, made us alive
together with Christ (by grace you have been
saved), and raised us up with Him, and seated
us with Him in the heavenly *places* in Christ
Jesus, so that in the ages to come He might show
the surpassing riches of His grace in kindness
toward us in Christ Jesus" (Ephesians 2:4-7).

A promise of being seated with Christ is a promise of
being called a friend of Christ, not only redeemed from sin,
but freed from the guilt of transgressions and placed in a seat
of honor. What a glorious promise!

"If we deny Him, He also will deny us. If we are faithless, He remains faithful, for He cannot deny Himself." These
final "if we" verses might alarm some. But rather than giving
a sense of dread, these twin phrases should evoke holy fear
and intense gratitude for the character and nature of God.

Jesus corroborated these verses in His earthly teaching
when He stated, "Therefore everyone who confesses Me
before men, I will also confess him before My Father who is
in heaven. But whoever denies Me before men, I will also deny
him before My Father who is in heaven" (Matthew 10:32-33).

Some Christians cite these verses as proof that believers
can lose their salvation, and that certain sins can re-sepa-
rate them from God. This, however, is a teaching that stands
opposed to the claims of Christ. He refutes this belief when
He assures believers, "My sheep hear My voice, and I know
them, and they follow Me; and I give eternal life to them, and
they will never perish; and no one will snatch them out of My

hand" (John 10:27-28). Many other verses in Scripture support the belief that a Christian, once saved is always saved.[80]

At a glance, the meaning of this verse seems a quandary. Paul, however, is not speaking of the loss of faith for a believer, but rather the actions of a non-believer. In the face of suffering, those who do not know Christ will deny Him and show their faithlessness. This is the nature of those not saved. Despite the volatile actions of an unbeliever, the truth of God's Word remains constant. He is Faithful. He is trustworthy. Those who He has declared righteous are acquitted forever. The Gospel is trustworthy because of the character of God's faithfulness.

You wouldn't expect encouragement from a condemned prisoner. You wouldn't anticipate words of hope from a man destined to die. However, these are the words and tone of Paul as he held out the Gospel truth—that Jesus Christ was enough. His resurrection from the dead promised the validity of the Gospel message, and the hope of Paul and Timothy and every subsequent believer.

This is the same hope believers cling to today. In a world of chaos and confusion, the power of the resurrection is still enough for us to face our tomorrows with courage. The glory of the risen Savior is still enough to allow us to mother with hope. These are truths we can rest on in the best and the worst of circumstances. As we keep our eyes fixed on Christ, we become deeply convicted that *He is enough,* and we dwell in the hope that only He can provide.

In what ways in your life might discipleship require self-denial?

_____

_____

_____

_____

_____

_____

_____

_____

_____

THIRTEEN

WISDOM FROM THE WORD

Remind them of these things, and solemnly charge them in the presence of God not to wrangle about words, which is useless and leads to the ruin of the hearers.

Be diligent to present yourself approved to God as a workman who does not need to be ashamed, accurately handling the word of truth.

But avoid worldly and empty chatter, for it will lead to further ungodliness, and their talk will spread like gangrene. Among them are Hymenaeus and Philetus, men who have gone astray from the truth saying that the resurrection has already taken place, and they upset the faith of some.

2 TIMOTHY 2:14-18

PEOPLE WILL SUE OVER anything. In 2005, a judge by the name of Roy Pearson filed a lawsuit against his dry cleaner for misplacing a pair of laundered pants. While the clothing was retrieved, he still pressed charges for $54 million to compensate for mental distress and inconvenience. The case went on for a considerable time, but finally the dry cleaners were awarded legal fees. They won the case, but the absurdity of the suit greatly tarnished their reputation.[81]

The news is littered with unwarranted lawsuits, each begging the question; why can't people get along? Unfortunately, followers of Jesus are often as guilty as non-Christians for this style of fractured living. We struggle to live in harmony with our families and friends just like everyone else. And as is so often characteristic of the Word of God, the passage in this chapter hits home with the besetting sin of disunity. Dysfunctional relationships are the fruit of divisive speech. "Remind them of these things," Paul begins the verse. After his exhortation to remember the worth of the Gospel and its worthiness regarding our suffering for it, Paul transitions to practical teaching for maintaining church unity.

Fighting about words is a never-ending battle, and if there is a sin we mamas fall victim to, word-sins are often it. Paul specifically addresses those who are saved to live with purity in speech; not forcing their way in every conversation; not needing the final word every time. He reiterates this concept in his letter to the Ephesian church:

> "Therefore I, the prisoner of the Lord, implore you to walk in a manner worthy of the calling with which you have been called with all humility and gentleness, with patience, showing tolerance for one another in love, being diligent to preserve the unity of the Spirit in the bond of peace" (Ephesians 4:1-3).

Bodies of Christ-followers should be characterized by a spirit of humility and a single-minded purpose that allows them to move forward in unity. Apparently, tendencies for disunity were as strong in the first century church as they are today, as Paul spent precious space in this brief letter to warn against it. He saw the ramifications for arguing and dissention as a disastrous—the original word he used literally means "catastrophic." The same word we use for hurricanes and floods and wildfires. He was well aware that words are dangerous.

So, what did Paul see as the antidote to this type of destructive speech? He turned to the integrity of the Word of God to safeguard speech and maintain purity in relationships between believers. Timothy was exhorted to diligent, skillful handling of the Word of God. This was not merely so that the church at Ephesus would have entertaining sermons or creative cross-references in their weekly meetings. Timothy was to become excellent in his handling of the Word so he could properly field issues in the church like divisive speech and arguing. Paul specifically highlighted the heretical teaching of two people in Timothy's circle who were spreading outright lies and damaging the health of the local church.

Scriptural literacy is the solution to refuting error and promoting unity in the church. Good doctrine breeds good morals. This is applicable in the first-century church, and in our modern-day homes as it elevates the platform for right living from our own preferences to the mandates of God. We can hold believers (and ourselves) to a higher standard of living when we recognize that we are serving a holy God. He calls us to "Be holy, for I AM holy" (1 Peter 1:16b). But how are we to do that if we don't know what "holy" is regarding ourselves, or what God expects?

How do we cultivate scriptural literacy when we are handicapped by limited resources and time? We *dwell* and we *dispel*. In our information-rich culture, we have opportunity to constantly learn. We can use various resource—be it the Bible, commentaries, studies—and dwell with the Lord. This exercise should come with a healthy dose of wisdom. We can either fill ourselves with good teaching so we can handle God's Word with excellence, or we can fill our minds with chatter. There is Christian teaching that is little more than idle talk—teaching based on opinion that does little to grow our worship for God or understanding of His character. This isn't helpful, and we need to guard against it.

We also dispel, which means we clean house and declutter. Any teaching we hold onto that is merely pandering to our feelings or keeping us from true growth, needs to go. We do this to focus in on what really matters, and to lead our children in a true and right understanding of God's Word. Only when we know God's Word can we understand the beautiful application it holds for our lives.

Do you live a life of unity, and are there relationships that you need to shore up to accomplish this? Explain:

_____

_____

_____

_____

_____

_____

_____

_____

_____

FOURTEEN

SEALED IN CHRIST

Nevertheless, the firm foundation of God stands,
having this seal, "The Lord knows those who
are His," and, "Everyone who names the name
of the Lord is to abstain from wickedness."

2 TIMOTHY 2:19

THERE IS A WORLD of difference between accomplished sculptors and novices. Those who begin the craft must practice patience. An unmeasured blow can quickly destroy a carving in granite or marble, and the artisan will face fewer of these disasters if he can exercise this skill.

First, he selects a piece of stone with the finished figurine already forged in his mind. Next, blow by careful blow, with each bit of chiseling, he brings the unformed mass into conformity with what he has mentally designed.

God is the Master Artist, crafting the lives of men and women into the likeness of His Son through the tiny strokes of sanctification. Scraping and polishing is His craftsmanship, wearing away at the vestiges of our sinful nature, allowing us to immerge as the final product He has always intended us to be.

Paul highlighted this doctrine—God's foreknowledge of the believer—encouraging Timothy that despite the heresy of false teachers and the divisiveness of empty talkers, God is faithful to preserve His church and protect His elect. The promise of this protection is His seal.

In the ancient world, the seal served as the legal signature of its owner. It was used for doing business or legalizing formal documents, and was synonymous with ownership. In these short chapters, Paul addressed the men who had done damage to the Ephesian church; men of whom he was warning Timothy to be wary. He advised against the deserters, Phygelus and Hermogenes. He cautioned regarding the dissenters; Hymenaeus and Philetus. Later, he mentions how Demas had disavowed him, and how Alexander had worked destruction against him.

In Paul's final days, these betrayals were a twisted knife in the heart of the aged apostle. Yet, he shows no concerns for the growth of church or the spread of the Gospel. Despite false teaching and the falling away of once-called believers, Paul was able to confidently rest in the assurance that the Lord's seal was on His people, and His church would not be shaken.

God knows believers by name, and those names are recorded in a book referred to throughout Scripture as the Book of Life. Jesus mentions this book explicitly in His revelatory message to the church at Sardis. "He who overcomes will thus be clothed in white garments; and I will not erase his name from the book of life, and I will confess his name before My Father and before His angels" (Revelation 3:5). The predestination of believers dictates their presence in this book, and protects them from apostasy.[82] Jesus reiterates this assurance to believers stating, "No one will snatch them out of My hand" (John 10:28b).

In a world of descending darkness, this truth ought to fill each mama's heart with the hope of glad expectancy. Like the rush of relief for a diagnosis dispelled or a financial crisis averted, we can rest in the hope that our babies' future is not dependent on the spiritual or political climate of the day. The firm foundation of God and His Gospel stands eternal. Believers in His name are secure—sealed. This is radical hope, unshaken by the worst our world has to offer. If our children are believers in Christ, then they are sealed in Him. We need not go through our lives fearful that our culture will have its way with them—with their precious souls or their minds. They are secure in God's hands.

This passage does not, however, give Timothy (or us) the permission for a laze faire faith. There is a clear directive tied to this promise of security—believers are to be holy.

Throughout the years, various studies have argued over what is considered safe levels of alcohol consumption for pregnant mothers. Some sources have contested that low consumption of alcoholic beverages throughout pregnancy offers negligible impact on the developing child. Despite these studies, authorities such as the American Academy of Pediatrics maintain a staunch position, stating "there is no safe level of alcohol use during pregnancy."[83]

What is required of pregnant mothers? Complete alcohol abstinence? I think that's a very prudent choice. While some believe there is "moderate sin" that we can tolerate, true Christians know that we can't give concessions for "safe sins." We are to be holy, mirroring God in every area of our lives.

As we raise our children, this means that our homes

should look different than that of nonbelievers. Holiness in our home means staying away from anything that would let sin through the front door. Vulgar speech needs to be ousted. Movies or shows that ridicule our beliefs or glorify immorality do nothing to encourage a lifestyle of holiness. Perhaps your family gossips about the neighbors or members of your small group. Whatever your circumstances, pursue holiness in your home.

Nonbelievers should be able to see the difference the minute they step inside, just as they should perceive something "peculiar" in those who are sealed with God's Holy Spirit. As we rest in the joy of being saved by Him, our natural response—as believers and as mothers—should be our obedience in lifestyle and virtue.

How does your position in Christ impact the way that you approach your duties as a mom, as a wife, or as a friend? Give an example:

_____

_____

_____

_____

FIFTEEN

FIT FOR GOOD USE

Now in a large house there are not only gold and silver vessels, but also vessels of wood and of earthenware, and some to honor and some to dishonor. Therefore, if anyone cleanses himself from these things, he will be a vessel for honor, sanctified, useful to the Master, prepared for every good work. Now flee from youthful lusts and pursue righteousness, faith, love and peace, with those who call on the Lord from a pure heart.

2 TIMOTHY 2:20-22

MANY WOMEN HAVE TWO collections of household decorations, pre-children and post-children. During the years of raising little ones, many women choose to swap their trendy knick-knacks and linen upholstery for unbreakable pieces and washable slipcovers. A small sacrifice to make, women give up their beautiful items to allow the smaller residents to enjoy their space freely, which in turn alleviates the constant fear for their safety and the destruction of property.

Most mamas don't begrudge a Lego creation adorning the mantle or a play-dough bakery on the kitchen table, but there is a silent understanding that these are *lesser* items. No woman would pass a designer home display and argue that the curated palate of colors and styles was inferior to her preschool-friendly living room. But there is a season for each.

Likewise, God's kingdom is comprised of simple and extravagant décor. Paul paints the picture of a grand house, perhaps a manor, filled with possessions of great quality. In this home, there are beautiful treasures we dream of having—items of great worth. They are for display and for use only in the most special of occasions. In this home, there are also the common items. There are wood and clay jars used for carrying water, storing food, and removing waste. These items are included in the house, but are regarded as less valuable, and given fewer desirable positions to fill.

This parable is a word picture that Paul used to help Timothy appreciate the value of holiness and sanctification within believers. The prior verses give attributes of a man who has no reason to be ashamed before the Lord. He is a man who handles the Word well, and uses his own words wisely. Paul illustrates the truth—that the unashamed workman lives in holiness so that he can be used in the highest capacity in God's house.

God isn't merely concerned that we serve Him *period*, but rather that we serve Him in *the right manner*. From the earliest recording of humans worshipping the Lord, God has a clear outline of actions and attitudes He expects for right worship. Cain and Abel, the first human brothers, both brought sacrifices to God. But He saw their hearts, and accepted one and rejected the other. Jesus even warns those who do good things in the name of God, but never truly have a relationship with Him.[84]

Similarly, believers can do many good things throughout their lives, and never strive to build the Kingdom of God. Paul warns the Corinthian church regarding this subject:

> "For no man can lay a foundation other than the one which is laid, which is Jesus Christ. Now if any man builds on the foundation with gold, silver, precious stones, wood, hay, straw, each man's work will become evident; for the day will show it because it is to be revealed with fire, and the fire itself will test the quality of each man's work. If any man's work which he has built on it remains, he will receive a reward." (1 Corinthians 3:11-14).

How do we as believers know if the work we're doing is for the Lord or for ourselves?

How can we avoid having all of our good works burned up, and how do we strive to be a beautiful, useful vessel in the Kingdom of God? Paul addresses these questions with two simple commands: Flee youthful lusts. Pursue righteousness.

As a younger man, likely somewhere in his thirties, Timothy was probably still susceptible to many of the pitfalls that trouble younger believers today. Pastor McArthur fleshes out these youthful lusts explaining, "These lusts involve much more than sinful sexual desire. They also include pride, craving for wealth and power, inordinate ambition, jealousy, envy, an argumentative and self-assertive spirit, and many other sinful lusts."[85]

How often do these wrong ambitions silently drive our desire (or lack of desire) to serve the Lord? How often do we serve God to leverage a better position in our church? Do we ever indulge our craving for self-assertion when we spout our Bible knowledge needlessly? Our sin nature can wriggle its way into how we pray, meet the needs of others, and even worship the Lord. Oh, how we need the blood of Jesus to make us holy, for we cannot do it ourselves! And yet Paul does not call Christians to a rigid form of asceticism as a safeguard from sin, but rather to run from sin and towards righteousness.

What does that look like? The wise handling of God's Word and our own. We can start by knowing God's Word and carefully evaluating where our words and actions don't match. We can apply this by asking the Lord for help, that our words and thoughts would line up with His standards. The writer of the Psalms set a model for this type of living when he wrote,

> "Set a guard, O LORD, over my mouth; Keep watch over the door of my lips. Do not incline my heart to any evil thing,
>
> To practice deeds of wickedness
>
> With men who do iniquity; And do not let me eat of their delicacies" (Psalm 141:3-4).

We live in an output-focused world, yet the Lord asks us to first develop the inward self. We cannot effectively *do* for the Lord until we have become the people He has called us to be. This doesn't mean that we put our lives on hold until we've reached some level of perfection, but it does mean we prioritize cultivating inward holiness as we serve those around us. As we root out sin and seek to mirror Christ, our actions will become purposeful, meaningful, and beautiful in the sight of God—as a mother and a believer.

Give an example of personal holiness in your life—what does it look like?

_____

_____

_____

_____

_____

_____

_____

_____

_____

SIXTEEN

HOLINESS IN WORD AND DEED

*But refuse foolish and ignorant speculations, knowing
that they produce quarrels. The Lord's bond-servant
must not be quarrelsome, but be kind to all, able
to teach, patient when wronged, with gentleness
correcting those who are in opposition, if perhaps
God may grant them repentance leading to the
knowledge of the truth, and they may come to
their senses and escape from the snare of the devil,
having been held captive by him to do his will.*

2 TIMOTHY 2:23-26

THE WORLD LOVES A good church scandal. Perhaps it's the sensationalism of a security threat, a videotaped committee meeting that went sideways and goes viral, or perhaps the embarrassing failure of a high-profile Christian who is obvious fuel for scrutiny.

As followers of Christ, some of us can also struggle with destroying the reputation of our church. We argue, we exclude, we criticize, thus giving the name of Jesus a bad connotation.

Paul repeated his warning for wisdom in words, telling the church in his letter to not squabble about words.[86] To refuse foolish and ignorant speculations. Not to fall into the trap of being argumentative or needing to be right, but rather to apply himself to knowledge of the Word. Paul began his exhortation with a direct imperative. "But refuse foolish and ignorant speculations, knowing that they produce quarrels." The original Greek used for foolish, *mōros*,[87] is the same root word for moron, coupled with the second descriptive word, *apaideutos*,[88] which carries the meaning of being without instruction or uneducated. Paul was commanding Timothy to avoid arguments that would do little more than make him appear to be an uneducated fool.

For Timothy, this was a particularly poignant prescription. While little is known of Timothy's speech habits, Scripture shares that he was in a position of power in the church, and that he was young. These were two prime reasons for him to avoid anything that could expose him to ridicule. With Paul's imminent death and the passing his spiritual mantle to Timothy, his speech would be under scrutiny. Nothing would discredit his witness more quickly than getting into meaningless verbal scrimmages.

Scripture makes clear that words of believers impact the witness of the Gospel. In the Book of Titus, Paul warns godly women to "Be reverent in their behavior, not malicious gossips nor enslaved to much wine, teaching what is good... so that the word of God will not be dishonored." (Titus 2:3b, 5b). Church leaders are outlined as being, "Above reproach, the husband of one wife, temperate, prudent, respectable, hospitable, able to teach, not.... pugnacious, but gentle, peaceable, free from the love of money" (1 Timothy 3:2b, 3b). All Christ followers are commanded to "Walk in a manner worthy of the calling with which you have been called, with all humility and gentleness, with patience, showing tolerance for one another in love, being diligent to preserve the unity of the Spirit in the bond of peace" (Ephesians 4:1-3). This manifold warning should serve as guideline that believers' speech matters.

Yet, we live in a time where what we say can often fall into one of two camps. First, we might err on the side of championing tolerance, and shy away from any controversies. Rather than addressing questionable ideas or sinful choices, we might affirm them or simply ignore them for the sake of keeping the peace. Conversely, we will plant plenty of flags in the ground that are impossible to misinterpret regarding our personal beliefs. Both extremes have pitfalls, but Paul taught a better way.

Timothy was not merely to avoid silly arguments; he was to know Scripture well enough that he could skillfully navigate conflict for the sake of the Gospel. As he worked to reconcile believers within the church, Timothy had the opportunity to reflect the image of Christ's reconciliation to those outside the church and offer them Gospel hope.

As mamas living in a world gone wrong, we should employ our words the same way in order to circumnavigate idle gossip and arguments that could destroy our Christian witness. We cultivate our witness through words not spoken as well as words shared. As King Solomon states in Proverbs 25:11, "Like apples of gold in settings of silver Is a word spoken in right circumstances."

As we are steeped in Scripture and meditation, we will be prone to sharing God's goodness and truth. As the Word of God transforms our heart by the renewing of our mind,[89] our thoughts are groomed for growth as our foundational roots instinctively reach out to others. This is what our children, and the watching world, need to see.

We live in a day and age that is starving for God's Word and its transformative power. Our children deserve mamas who don't fight to be right when it comes to trivial things. They need mamas who know Scripture and will teach it to them, showing by example how it is the only reasonable road-map to peace and security. As their mamas, we can choose our battles wisely, and always be ready for conflict with grace and a well-spoken word.

We are citizens of heaven living in a foreign place. As such, we are needed in this broken world now more than ever. Let us take this opportunity to be life-givers as we pursue verbal wisdom and holiness.

Are your words characterized as life-giving to your children? Your family? How so?

_____

_____

_____

_____

SEVENTEEN

READY FOR BATTLE

But realize this, that in the last days difficult times will come. For men will be lovers of self, lovers of money, boastful, arrogant, revilers, disobedient to parents, ungrateful, unholy, unloving, irreconcilable, malicious gossips, without self-control, brutal, haters of good, treacherous, reckless, conceited, lovers of pleasure rather than lovers of God, holding to a form of godliness, although they have denied its power; Avoid such men as these.

2 TIMOTHY 3:1-5

SOME FOLKS MIGHT SAY that morality is relative to each individual. As Christians, we see people all around us that have very few morals, and they feel no sense of shame or guilt. But you and I know that society needs moral absolutes to avoid anarchy. As President John Adams once said, "Our constitution was made only for a moral and religious people. It is wholly inadequate to the government of any other."[90] His reasoning is sound. How can one work for the advancement of life and liberty if one can't first admit that all people are created equal? How does a country work towards justice and tranquility if there is not some common understanding of the ethos of right and wrong?

These notably absent absolutes mark our culture today, and are evident of the difficult times that Paul prophesied about—that followers of Jesus would inevitably find themselves navigating. Paul warned Timothy to be on guard against the immorality that would become increasingly pervasive. As a beacon of righteousness and truth, Christ-followers would become a target by those committed to atheism, syncretism, and pantheism.

The Roman people worshipped a multiplicity of gods, and believed in a subjective concept of morality. The infant church of Jesus stood up in the face of enormous cultural pushback. This was one of many reasons why Christians were hated, persecuted, and killed—they threatened the way of life that was comfortable to a thriving world superpower.

In his letter to Timothy, Paul outlined a culture that had turned its back on God's standards. He crafted a similar list in his letter to the Roman church, stating that people who didn't acknowledge God experienced a personal implosion, propelled by moral decay.

"And just as they did not see fit to acknowledge God any longer, God gave them over to a depraved mind, to do those things which are not proper, being filled with all unrighteousness, wickedness, greed, evil; full of envy, murder, strife, deceit, malice; they are gossips, slanderers, haters of God, insolent, arrogant, boastful, inventors of evil, disobedient to parents, without understanding, untrustworthy, unloving, unmerciful; and although they know the ordinance of God, that those who practice such things are worthy of death, they not only do the same, but also give hearty approval to those who practice them" (Romans 1:28-32).

What was the reason for Paul's meticulous outline for the character of a fallen people? He was introducing Timothy to his reality as a minister of the Gospel, and a spokesman for right and wrong. Jesus offered a succinct warning when he said, "Behold, I send you out as sheep in the midst of wolves; so be shrewd as serpents and innocent as doves" (Matthew 10:16).

Paul's charge to Timothy was to be on the alert and able to identify the wolves in disguise. They not only were propagating wrong behaviors, but they were peddling wrong ideas. Paul warned of these people, saying, "[they hold] to a form of godliness, although they have denied its power" (2 Timothy 3:5a). These were people who could inflict the most confusion and damage to the church. They were men who claimed some level of spirituality, but were anything but followers of Christ.

We see this same cultural pattern in our society today. Men and women love being called religious, and acknowledge the benefits of morality while rejecting the exclusivity of trusting in Jesus Christ's salvation work on the Cross. Grace has become an empty word as sin has been scrubbed from our vocabulary. For those who want the assurance of a happy life—freedom from responsibility and a promised place in heaven—many so-called teachers have rebranded Christianity.

That is, holding to a form of godliness, but not one that God has designed or accepts.

The prosperity Gospel teachers—progressive Christianity teachers and others—have gone out of their way to make God accommodating to the cultural flavors of the day. But Scripture warns that God has ready judgment for these heretical teachings.

"And in their greed they will exploit you with false words; their judgment from long ago is not idle, and their destruction is not asleep" (2 Peter 2:3).

Successful battles are fought by soldiers who have prepared. Those who are casualties don't know how to use their weapons, or are unfamiliar with war-time strategy. Paul was outlining the battlefield in which Timothy would fight. He was calling him to advance for the sake of the Gospel, mindful of the challenges that he would face. He was warning him so he could be assured of victory, rather than overwhelmed by the obstacles.

We are called to the same challenge. You and I can help prepare our children to engage in a daily-mounting Spiritual battle. We do this by first knowing Scripture, and also by helping our children identify the reality of it in the world around them. As we see our society sprinting away from the truths of God's Word, rampant greed, self-centeredness, hatred, and violence becomes increasingly prevalent. We are wise to acknowledge these challenges, and identify Scripture as the only absolute in a world of vanishing absolutes. We also do this by carefully filtering any biblical teaching we ingest—whether in church, through a podcast, or television programs. We ought to be ready to fact-check teaching against

God's Word for accuracy and truth. We are wise to teach our children to do the same.

Finally, there is a time to cut ties with those who are detrimental to our faith. Paul cautioned Timothy in this way, and his warning is worth heeding. The purity of the Gospel will never be tainted by the testimony of one witness, but that one witness is capable of turning an unbeliever from the truth. Therefore, ready yourself for battle, well able to outline the truth and fight for it.

For the sake of our children's faith.

For the advancement of the Gospel!

What are ways you can prepare to stand up to false teaching and ideas for the spiritual well-being of your little ones?

_____

_____

_____

_____

_____

EIGHTEEN

DON'T BE THAT WOMAN

*For among them are those who enter into households
and captivate weak women weighed down with
sins, led on by various impulses, always learning and
never able to come to the knowledge of the truth.*

*Just as Jannes and Jambres opposed Moses,
so these men also oppose the truth, men of
depraved mind, rejected in regard to the faith.*

*But they will not make further progress; for
their folly will be obvious to all, just as Jannes's
and Jambres's folly was also.*

2 TIMOTHY 3:6-9

WOMEN WHO COMPETE IN the Miss America pageant are subject to the highest standards of excellence. For the competition, they must be eloquent, poised, and affable. For over one hundred years, this annual contest is held to crown the most beautiful woman in the country, with the underlying sub-message that beauty is more than just looks. It is also decorum. While thousands of women have shone in this competitive pageant, most spectators have reveled over the failures. Each botched interview or clumsy misstep has been revisited by the public for careful criticism.

While it would be terribly embarrassing to be immortalized by an empty response to an important question, how much more detrimental to have your testimony tarnished by being a woman lacking discernment?

Paul spent considerable time outlining the dangers of the last days, and the characteristics of a people who had rejected orthodoxy to follow God however they pleased. The result of their apostasy was all sorts of self-centered and dangerous living, which he carefully outlined to Timothy. He also cautioned that Timothy should be especially attentive to a particularly vulnerable group: silly women.

This verse has caused offense to some. Many women bristle at their sex being called out in such an unflattering way. However, context begs the reader to take her pulse and remember that this passage was not originally written for women to read. It was written from Paul to Timothy, and included this series of final instructions for the safety and longevity of the church. This passage was not for the belittlement of women in general, but rather for their good.

The original Greek word literally means "a little [implying foolish] woman."[91] Proverbs states that, "The woman of folly is boisterous, she is naïve and knows nothing" (Proverbs 9:13). This silly woman is one who speaks without knowledge, quick to air her opinions without knowing what she's saying. The word choice in this passage also carries the connotation of a person who is volatile and angered, speaking in a rash or emotional way. In short, this foolish woman is a wrecking ball.

Proverbs goes on to say, "The wise woman builds her house, but the foolish tears it down with her own hands"

DON'T BE THAT WOMAN

(Proverbs 14:1). Perhaps this destruction is through her unmeasured words or impulsive actions. Whatever the case, in her wake lies ruin. These are words that are easy to skim past, but given flesh and bones, they carry weight. Real women in real homes ruin their family bond through impulsive words and actions. Women who cannot guard their tongue or control their emotions, disrupt the harmony in their home, and can destroy relationships and even their reputation. These are women who are vulnerable to being deceived because they are not grounded; they lack the discernment to recognize their own naivety.

Paul was telling Timothy to be on the alert for women who were particularly vulnerable to attack; those who were ignorant of the Gospel, doctrine, and therefore defenseless against the errant teaching of heretics. Women who were in deep trouble and didn't even know it.

This serious warning was paired with hope, offered with a portrait of the past. Paul outlined the folly of two men, Jannes and Jambres, whose names are otherwise absent from Scripture. Using cultural and historical clues, many scholars agree that these men were the Egyptian priests who mimicked the miracles of Moses prior to the Exodus of the Israelite people. They were successful in working some of the signs of Moses, turning their staffs into serpents, water into blood, and summoning frogs upon the land[92] But the power of the two men was finite. They could not conjure up locusts, command darkness, send hail, or orchestrate the annihilation of Egypt's firstborn.

These worshippers of false gods came to the realization of God's reality and His miracles in Egypt, even confessing His power displayed in the signs of Moses.[93]

Paul referenced these individuals to show the limited power that evil will have on the Church of Christ. In the day of Moses, Jannes and Jambres must have caused difficulty. As they duplicated the very signs Moses used to validate his message, they were surely the source of much discouragement and frustration in the heart of God's messenger. But God was not shaken by their slithering staffs or water-turned-blood. He had established the release of His people, and there was nothing Jannes and Jambres or Pharoh or anyone else could do stop Him. Paul reminded Timothy of this historical vignette to reassure him of God's continued plan for His church. The Church of Jesus could not truly be shaken by false teachers. There might be women (and men) who would buy into the deception, but the truth of the Gospel would always stand.

Paul's warning to Timothy was not written to us, but we can glean from its message. As women who follow Christ, we have the duty to practice discernment with all that we ingest, and that we feed our children. We cannot blithely follow internet teachers and purchase Scripture resources hoping they will serve to build us up. There are false teachers vying for the hearts (and money) of women who want nothing more than to learn something new. Let us be wise so as not to fall for these schemes.

We do this by saturating ourselves with Scripture—Scripture in context—so we can identify and refute false teaching. We protect ourselves by talking to wise and discerning family members, ideally our saved husbands, and seeking their counsel for questions about the Word that we do not understand. If a single mother, when we come to a difficult passage, we enter God's throne room in humility, and ask the Lord to reveal His truth. May the response of Charles Spurgeon resonate in our hearts as we approach Scripture.

> "If you are afraid for yourselves, I am not afraid for you. If you tremble at God's Word, you have one of the surest marks of God's elect."[94]

May we be humble and wise, instructed by the Word through the Holy Spirit, so that we can live with discernment in this dark world.

What might this humble posture look like in your life?

_____

_____

_____

_____

_____

_____

NINETEEN

FAITH-FILLED SERVANT, FAITHFUL MASTER

*Now you followed my teaching, conduct,
purpose, faith, patience, love, perseverance,
persecutions, and sufferings, such as happened
to me at Antioch, at Iconium and at Lystra;
what persecutions I endured, and out of them
all the Lord rescued me! Indeed, all who desire to
live godly in Christ Jesus will be persecuted. But
evil men and impostors will proceed from
bad to worse, deceiving and being deceived.*

2 TIMOTHY 3:10-13

IN THE MID-EIGHTEEN HUNDREDS, unacclaimed hymn writer Edward Mote penned the words to one of the most influential songs in Christendom. The young Englishman had lived for self and pleasure until the cabinetmaker to whom he was apprenticed took him to church, and there he was affronted with the truth of the Gospel. His life changed, and one day in his cabinet shop, God gave him the words to the beloved hymn, *The Solid Rock*. This song first ministered to the dying wife of one of Mote's friends, and has since reached generations with the timeless truths of God's unchanging faithfulness. One of the hope-filled stanzas reads as follows:

> "When darkness veils His lovely face I rest on His
> unchanging grace. In every high and stormy gale
> My anchor holds within the veil."

The anchor holds. Although written almost two centuries after the life of the Apostle Paul, the hymn still echoes the theme God's faithfulness as seen in this saint's life. In this passage especially, Paul reminds Timothy that the faithfulness of God is not impacted by circumstance, but in the constant Spirit that buoyed his life.

Paul reminded Timothy of the high cost of following Christ, which Paul exemplified. Since the beginning of Paul's teaching ministry, the responses to his instruction had been a milieu of acceptance and rejection, often followed by a flurry of persecution. He recalled three specific locations where his faithful service to Christ had led to persecution.

Antioch was the origin of Paul's initial missionary journey. There, he partnered with Barnabas, and began ministering to Jews and God-fearing Greeks. While at first, there was a good response to their message, but shortly after, some of the Jews caused an uproar, contradicting the words of Paul and blaspheming, speaking evil of the apostle. This dissention culminated in the Jews driving the apostles from the area. But God used this setback to pivot Paul's ministry to be focused primarily on the Gentiles.[95]

Following the mistreatment in Antioch, the apostles fled to Iconium where they spoke with boldness until an attempt was made to stone them by the Jews and the Greeks. Fleeing the violence in Iconium, they traveled to Lystra where they healed a lame man then proclaimed by the residents as gods. The apostles worked feverishly to quell this false belief, and with the help of angry Jews, the mob turned from idolizing the pair to wanting to kill them.

Paul was stoned and dragged outside the city, assumed to be dead. Through a miraculous recovery, he not only survived, but was revived enough to travel with Barnabas the following day.[96]

What was the purpose to revisiting these difficult episodes in ministry? Paul was illustrating the truth to Timothy. "Indeed, all who desire to live godly in Christ Jesus will be persecuted" (2 Timothy 3:12). This wasn't an idle observation. He used his life as an illustration to show his young friend that faithful service is costly, and opposition should be expected and, perhaps, even deadly.

From his cell in the ground, Paul surveyed the culture—both the false teachers and the pagan leaders—and acknowledged that from appearances, evil held all the cards. But in the dark hour of Paul's final days, he underscored this warning with a recurrent hope. Antioch, Iconium, and Lystra, had been filled with difficulty, yet in the midst of trial, Paul saw the hand of God moving in his ministry, and cultivating fruit out of hard circumstances. Paul even had this expectation of his current station in Rome: "The Lord will rescue me from every evil deed, and will bring me safely to His heavenly kingdom" (2 Timothy 4:18a).

Paul was quick to recount the faithfulness of God, and to encourage Timothy that where God had been faithful before, He would be faithful again.

There are few wonders like the night sky deep in the

country. A blanket of black spans the horizon, pierced by an array of pin-points of light. Miles from cell phone towers or the distraction of headlights, tiny bursts of starlight penetrate the emptiness, pushing away the darkness. Our testimonies where God has intervened are like the starlight in a silent sky. In a world where evil seems to permeate every crevice of our culture, we have the opportunity to be truth-bearers that God is still at work.

Like Paul, we have stories of God's faithfulness, too. If we have been saved from our sins by Jesus and given new life, each new day is a testimony to that faithfulness. If you used to live bogged down in sin, and God has given you victory, you have a story to tell. If you have prayed for a wayward child, and seen repentance in their heart, you can celebrate the won-der-working power of God. These are stories that we need to share. We have opportunity to poke holes in the darkness and let the Gospel light of God's Word shine through. Our families need this reminder. Our children need this reminder. The generation in despair about the future, and the generations that will walk in it, need to know that God still rescues. He still saves. He is still at work.

Can you think of a time in your life when God was the anchor you desperately needed? In what way did He ground you?

_____

_____

_____

_____

_____

_____

_____

_____

TWENTY

THE SUFFICIENCY OF SCRIPTURE

*You, however, continue in the things you have
learned and become convinced of, knowing from
whom you have learned them, and that from
childhood you have known the sacred writings
which are able to give you the wisdom that leads
to salvation through faith which is in Christ Jesus.*

2 TIMOTHY 3:14-15

PEOPLE WILL GO TO great lengths to lose weight.
Among some of the more drastic diet programs, some have
eaten tapeworms (as awful as that sounds) in hopes that the
parasite will eat their food for them. Others have dabbled
in eliminating major food groups, going either completely
carnivore or completely vegan. Some experiment with inter-
mittent fasting combined with massive meals in between.
Some budget for expensive makeover surgeries that promise
instant, lasting results. Online influencers and stars with the
"it factor" vouch for the effectiveness of each technique, so

people try them in hopes that it will change their lives, giving them the body they desire.

Despite the flurry of trending weight-loss options, health care providers continue to advocate for the traditional methods of a balanced diet, adequate sleep, and frequent exercise. Yet people still continue the search for something newer. Something trendier. Something endorsed by beautiful people. And much like our desire for something new in the health world, we want something fresh in our faith journeys. This is where false teachers are able to snag unsuspecting women who are eager to always learn something new. It can be a trap.

In Paul's letter to Timothy, he gives a directive: to remain. In the verses prior to this, He warns of the torrent of sins and difficulties Timothy should expect as he saw a society turning to flagrant sin. In the midst of false doctrine, in the face of fleshly indulgence, Timothy was to stand as an immovable partition between right and wrong. Paul didn't require Timothy to become versed in every errant teacher's ideology. He wasn't to brush up on the latest debate tactics. He was to steep himself in the truths of God's Word, and to allow those truths to guide his responses regarding false teaching, to sin, and to persecution.

Paul highlighted Timothy's acquisition of these truths in sequential order, showing the faith journey that had culminated in this young pastor's leadership role. Timothy had learned the Word as a child. The original word Paul uses implies that he was taught from before he was born.[97] Timothy's believing mother and grandmother had clearly taken their calling to disciple him seriously. From his earliest days, they were presenting him with the Word, likely familiarizing him with the major stories from the Old Testament, highlighting the character of God. Their teaching was rewarded when Timothy eventually became convinced of the truth.

Somewhere along the way, teaching was no longer an academic exercise for Timothy; it was real. This conviction of truth also propelled his understanding for a personal need for a Savior, resulting in his salvation.

Timothy was grounded in the truth since childhood. But this spiritual teaching was meant to be much more than a pedigree. It was his defense against a world gone wrong. In a place opposed to the things of God, Paul was reminding Timothy of his need to draw upon his teaching, to grow deep in his walk with the Lord, and to remain immovable against whatever difficulties came his way.

Health professionals advocate for the importance of reading aloud to children to support their cognitive and emotional development. Even the youngest of children benefit from the one-on-one attention of this simple pastime, and studies show that reading to an infant helps to facilitate their school readiness by kindergarten.[98]

Parents understand the need to support children's cognitive development to help them grow. It only makes sense that from their infancy, we should support their spiritual development, as well.

There is so much value in reading Scripture to the smallest of children, even before they can make sense of the words. The importance of what's read is imprinted on their hearts. Songs are also powerful vehicles of teaching and memorizing Scripture through music. It is a wonderful way to begin the discipleship process at the earliest age. The old hymns like *A Mighty Fortress is Our God* and *What a Friend We Have in Jesus* teaches the truths about God's character and nature in a way that is easily grasped. Contemporary artists have set Scripture to song, making memorization a simple thing. These are tools that any one of us moms can use.

We live in an age like Paul's, where the sheer quantity of false teaching is staggering, and the opposition to truth is remarkable. We might feel powerless to protect our children against the dark world we are raising them in, but the responsibility is ours with each passing day to prepare them for the challenges we know they will face.

We do this through daily discipleship and our commitment to prayer. As evil relentlessly moves against our children, we cannot respond passively. Scripture says that, "The effective prayer of a righteous man can accomplish much" (James 5:16b). Let us commit to daily intercession for the spiritual wellbeing of our children. We can pray for them fervently, specifically, and purposefully, as if their lives depended on it. Because they do. God is eager to hear the faith-filled prayers of His children. That's *you*.

We can also help equip our children for their futures by doing just as Timothy's mother and grandmother did. We can teach our children the Word—actively and passively—by modeling a lifestyle of prioritizing the Bible, and through daily teaching and leading in the Word of God. Though we can never stay abreast of all the challenges that our culture will inflict on the faith of our children, but we can arm them with truth. We can prepare them by grounding them in the Word of God, and bathing them in prayer.

God's Word was sufficient to sustain Timothy in an era of hellish persecution. It can certainly withstand the challenges of today. Remain in the truth, Mama. Always.

In what ways do you believe your prayers can make an impact on the life of your child?

_____

_____

_____

_____

_____

_____

_____

_____

TWENTY ONE

EQUIPPED

*All Scripture is inspired by God and is profitable
for teaching, for reproof, for correction, for training
in righteousness, so that the man of God may
be adequate, equipped for every good work.*

2 TIMOTHY 3:16-17

IN THE LATE 17TH century, the world was gifted with a
brilliant German composer named Johan Sebastian Bach.
When Bach was orphaned at ten years of age, he moved to live
with his elder brother who was employed as a church organist.
Eventually, Bach's musical talent allowed him to begin earning
a living, first as a musician in the Weimar orchestra, then
serving as the organist for a church in Arnstadt, Germany.

A prolific composer, Bach also began writing sacred
and secular music. Many of his pieces were written in the
baroque style, which was very popular for his time. As one
of the greatest composers that ever lived, he posthumously
shaped the talent of countless contemporary composers that
would mimic his style. Over three hundred years after his
death, musicians worldwide are challenged and thrilled by
the brilliant compositions of this great man.[99]

Bach was inspired in a way few musicians can boast.

The dictionary definition of inspiration is "outstanding or brilliant in a way or to a degree suggestive of divine inspiration."[100] Often, the layperson's definition is "you know it when you see it." It is witnessed in a stunning performance, an impassioned speech, a tenacious athlete. Those who inspire often do so due to their greatness in their field and the way in which their excellence demands repetition.

In this chapter's pivotal passage, Paul points to the inspiration of the Word of God, and assures Timothy of its sufficiency to guide him after Paul's death.

All Scripture Is God-Breathed

Written less than seventy years after the resurrection of Christ, this letter was received in a time where the cannon of Scripture was not yet closed. The Jewish people had long revered the Old Testament as the inspired words of God; a fact that Jesus affirmed by quoting Scripture repeatedly throughout His earthly ministry.[101] The Pharisees and Sadducees—the religious and legal leaders of Jesus' day—challenged His authoritative approach to the Word of God. Jesus addressed their objections this way:

> "Do not think that I came to abolish the Law or the Prophets; I did not come to abolish but to fulfill. For truly I say to you, until heaven and earth pass away, not the smallest letter or stroke shall pass from the Law until all is accomplished" (Matthew 5:17-18).

The Old Testament served as the covenant between God and His chosen people. It outlined the sin nature of man, born in the Garden of Eden, and was imprinted on every generation since. It gave a faint glimmer of a promised Messiah who would one day save humankind from its sins. Then Jesus came. The Apostle John explained Jesus like this: "The Word beca me flesh, and dwelt among us, and we saw His glory, glory as of the only begotten from the Father, full of grace and truth" (John 1:14).

Jesus is not only the substitute for our sin; He is also our way to know God. John writes, "No one has seen God at any time; the only begotten God who is in the bosom of the Father, He has explained Him" (John 1:18). Jesus' earthly ministry was characterized by his teaching, which focused often on the central themes of the Kingdom of God[102] and justification before Him.[103] Jesus' teaching was memorable, often delivered through parables or using literary devices such as hyperbole, to help His messages stick in the mind of the listener.

When Jesus ascended to heaven after His resurrection, the words that He spoke became the training manual for His disciples, and the blueprint for the early church.[104] Jesus even promised divine intervention on recall—that Holy Spirit would serve to help the disciples. "But the Advocate, the Holy Spirit, whom the Father will send in my name, will teach you all things and will remind you of everything I have said to you" (John 14:26).

Timothy was charged to employ the Old Testament Scripture he'd learned from childhood, as well as the teachings of Christ handed down to him by Paul. He was made privy to a wide swath of the epistles, assisting in writing many of the Pauline letters. These letters were received as divinely inspired, and were used for teaching, for reproof, and for training in righteousness. This was Timothy's seminary library as he labored to grow the infant church in the first century.

Profitable

Paul encouraged Timothy that the Word of God is profitable, implying that it is the sustenance of the believer. It is profitable for the training and equipping of the saints. It is the means by which the Gospel is reproduced and received in the hearts of believers. Theologian John MacArthur described the profitability of Scripture by stating, "Profitable translates *ōphelimos*, which includes the ideas of beneficial, productive and sufficient. Scripture is sufficient in being comprehensive. Paralleled in the Old Testament only by Psalm 119 and confirmed by Joshua 1:8, these verses supremely affirm the absolute sufficiency of Scripture to meet all the spiritual and physical needs of God's people."[105]

The profitability of the Scripture meant well-being for the people of Israel. Throughout Scripture, the wellbeing of the Israelites correlated directly to their obedience to the Law of the Lord.[106] Disaster overtook them when they turned from it. The Psalmist David understood and celebrated the sufficiency of the Scripture, writing in Psalm 119 of its immense value,[107] saying that the law of the Lord was his delight,[108] his source of wisdom,[109] and direction.[110]

Jesus taught that the Word of God, when planted in a receptive heart, had power to produce fruit a hundred-fold of what was sown.[111] In the Book of Acts, the early church was suffering persecution, but the writer comments that in the face of these circumstances, "the word of the Lord continued to grow and to be multiplied" (Acts 12:24b). The writer of Hebrews aptly stated, "For the word of God is living and active and sharper than any two-edged sword, and piercing as far as the division of soul and spirit, of both joints and marrow, and able to judge the thoughts and intentions of the heart" (Hebrews 4:12). The profitability of Scripture dictates that God's Word does not return void, which is declared in the Book of Isaiah:

> "For as the rain and the snow come down from heaven,
>
> And do not return there without watering the earth...
>
> So will My word be which goes forth from My mouth; It will not return to Me empty, Without accomplishing what I desire" (Isaiah 55:10a-11).

The Word of God is the believer's substance, and the source of great good for our lives.

Adequate

Additionally, the Apostle Paul encourages Timothy that the Word of God allows for adequacy in every good work. The word that Paul uses is *artios*, which means being "complete or perfect."[112] The word is used only once in the Bible, but it carries the idea of having aptitude for specific reasons. It is the same concept seen in the Book of 1 Samuel, when David went to kill Goliath. The king, Saul, wanted to outfit David with his armor, but the young warrior declined the offer. He was confident in his God and in his training. Armed with little more than these, he bested the Philistine champion. David, a shepherd boy, was adequate for the task at hand.

Paul did not know what God had for Timothy after his death. Many prominent Christ-followers in that day were stoned, crucified, or beheaded. Incarceration was also common. Paul couldn't predict Timothy's future, but he could prepare him for it. He did this by pointing Timothy to the profitability and the sustainability of the Scripture.

It was God's Word that would live on after Paul's death, and after Timothy's as well. One can only wonder if Paul could predict that his letters to Timothy would one day become Scripture itself. Turns out, it would span time from the first century to today, where this letter reaches women across the world.

Like Paul, women today have no ability to guess what challenges their children or grandchildren might face. In a world of abject immorality and senseless violence, we are offered the same hope the Apostle Paul clung to. The sustaining power of God's Word.

What relevance does this passage hold in your life? Perhaps you are in a season of empty-nesting. You can dedicate hours to studying God's Word, meditating on it, and praying God's promises over your young adult children. If this is your season, savor this as a blessing—a gift you can give to your kids.

If you find yourself in a twilight season where you no longer have children or grandchildren in your circle, encourage younger women and mothers to grow in the Word. Pray for them, and encourage them with Scripture. You might be God's answer to a very real need they have. Don't discount yourself from taking part in God's plan to disciple and mentor through His Word.

Perhaps you are in a season where small hands grab at

your Bible and spill your coffee every time you try to read. In this period, God's Word is profitable for you, too. As you make sacrifices to steal away a few private moments with the Lord, you subconsciously communicate the importance of His Word to your little ones. As you meditate on a snippet of verse while you do the dishes or quell a fight, you practice obedience to the Lord just by having His words abiding in your mind.

In whatever season you find yourself, His Word is sufficient to equip, sustain, and train you to live as the mama He has called you to be.

Are you seeing your heart and actions transformed by the word of God? In what ways?

_____

_____

_____

_____

_____

_____

TWENTY TWO

ARMED WITH TRUTH

I solemnly charge you in the presence of God and of Christ Jesus, who is to judge the living and the dead, and by His appearing and His kingdom: preach the word; be ready in season and out of season; reprove, rebuke, exhort, with great patience and instruction. For the time will come when they will not endure sound doctrine; but wanting to have their ears tickled, they will accumulate for themselves teachers in accordance to their own desires, and will turn away their ears from the truth and will turn aside to myths. But you, be sober in all things, endure hardship, do the work of an evangelist, fulfill your ministry.

2 TIMOTHY 4:1-5

A YOUNG WOMAN TOOK the American Red Cross CPR training course multiple times. She originally entered the class because her work required it. She sat at a table, mildly engaged. Her hands-on practice was half-hearted as she secretly willed the time to pass more quickly. Four years later, the woman enrolled in a CPR class again. Her family had relocated to a rural ranch, and her toddler had nearly choked on multiple occasions. The woman realized her competence in life-saving measures could mean the life of her child. This time, she stepped into the class almost desperate to learn. When she came to the role-play portion of the workshop, she kept envisioning her daughter's face as the compressions were absorbed by the CPR manikin.

In each case, the training was exactly the same, but the efficacy with which the material was received differed entirely. The mother realized the urgency of the message, and her need to master it.

Stepping into the last chapter of 2 Timothy, the reader can become disengaged, much like the mother in the anecdote. It is a passage of Scripture in which we can't easily place ourselves. It seems detached from our lives, and we might wonder if it is applicable by superimposing our teen or our toddler over the list of people unwilling to listen to sound doctrine. But things aren't quite that bleak. Let's start within the context of this book—as the words were first penned.

A Time to Speak

I solemnly charge you in the presence of God and of Christ Jesus, who is to judge the living and the dead, and by His appearing and His kingdom: preach the word.

2 TIMOTHY 4:1-2A

For years, their work had been entwined. The church at Ephesus, pastored by Timothy, was planted by Paul. This was a church tended by the apostle with relentless labor and emotional investment. In the Book of Acts, Paul outlines his ministry to this church in a heartfelt goodbye to the elders while having divine knowledge that this was his final farewell to this body of believers. He mentions the difficulty of his ministry in Ephesus, stating that he served with tears and trials,[113] and despite the challenges, his ministry was characterized by diligence in sharing all that the believers would need.[114]

In his farewell address, the Apostle Paul offered this benediction to the elders at Ephesus:

> "And now I commend you to God and to the word of His grace, which is able to build you up and to give you the inheritance among all those who are sanctified" (Acts 20:24).

Paul entrusted the church to the Word of God and to God Himself. He knew the Gospel would stand even after his death. And in his final instructions to Timothy, he returned to the necessity of maintaining God's Word, in all its integrity and purity.

In his final days on this earth, concern for the young preacher and his fledgling church occupied Paul's mind. Timothy was a true believer and faithful servant, yet he seemed to be waning in enthusiasm and zeal. A scholar by the name of Michael Brown summarizes the reason for Paul's concern:

> "Although he was Paul's most faithful and trusted colleague, Timothy was young, timid, frequently ill, and in need of encouragement. He faced a situation in the church of Ephesus that caused him to feel that he was in over his head. Persuasive false teachers were launching attacks on the

gospel. Some in the church were questioning his authority as a pastor. Moreover, he was perhaps embarrassed about Paul's imprisonment and declining reputation. He needed to stand up for the truth and faithfully preach the Word of God, but he was afraid of suffering."[115]

Paul understood the darkness of the hour, and the need for the light of the Gospel to shine in the church. More than anything, he wanted Timothy to feel that urgency as well.

Those who love sports movies can picture this familiar image; the rallying words of a coach to his team at half-time, in a game of seemingly overwhelming odds. In these films, the deflated team is revived with the impassioned belief of their coach that they can still win. These verses were Paul's final rally cry. Things appeared impossible for the church—heresy was rampant, and persecution pervasive. Yet Paul saw the final scoreboard. He knew Jesus had already won. And so, he called Timothy to press on in faithful service.

With Both Eyes on Eternity

I solemnly charge you in the presence of
God and of Christ Jesus, who is to judge the
living and the dead, and by His appearing
and His kingdom: preach the word.

2 TIMOTHY 4:1-2A

Paul called upon Timothy to live in faithfulness motivated by Christ's omnipotence and omnipresence. Scripture is explicit on Christ's position as the Judge of all mankind.[116] The verb used in this passage, *krinō*, carries multiple meanings, including to separate, to approve, and to judge. Three separate judgments are also taught in Scripture: the separation of sheep and goats,[117] the great white throne of judgement for unbelievers,[118] and the bema seat for believers.[119]

In this context, Paul was referencing Christ's final judgement of believers, appraising the works of saints for reward. He writes on this topic in his second letter to the Corinthian church, stating, "For we must all appear before the judgment seat of Christ, so that each one may be recompensed for his deeds in the body, according to what he has done, whether good or bad" (2 Corinthians 5:10). It seems Timothy had his eyes on the world, and on all the reasons why following Christ was difficult. For this reason, Paul used these verses to lift his protégés' eyes to heaven, where Jesus occupies the right hand of the Father, watching Timothy, witnessing his labors, fully aware of his ministry. What an encouragement.

Paul's Christ-ward focus inspired Timothy, that he belonged to Christ. His Judge was Christ, and his defender was Christ. Nothing he suffered would be forgotten. Being reminded of Christ's identity as the Eternal Judge would spur Timothy on to continued obedience.

A World Unraveling

Be ready in season and out of season; reprove, rebuke, exhort, with great patience and instruction. For the time will come when they will not endure sound doctrine; but wanting to have their ears tickled, they will accumulate for themselves teachers in

*accordance to their own desires, and will turn away
their ears from the truth and will turn aside to
myths. But you, be sober in all things, endure hardship,
do the work of an evangelist, fulfill your ministry.*

2 TIMOTHY 4:2B-5

In the Book of Deuteronomy, the Lord severely warned the people of Israel the dangers of mixing His commands with their own religious agenda. "Whatever I command you, you shall be careful to do; you shall not add to nor take away from it" (Deuteronomy 12:32). And yet, through the centuries, God's people have fallen for the dangers of syncretism.

In the early church, it was the legalistic Jews trying to coerce believers to hold to the laws of Moses in addition to their newfound faith in Christ.[120] Not many years ago, teachings of the Prosperity Gospel crept into the church, instilling that physical health and financial prosperity are blessings Christians are to expect. The Progressive Christianity movement also gained traction in recent years, deconstructing and questioning almost every tenet essential to the Christian faith. The brand of heresy is little more than tired lies re-peddled by the Evil One. The believer must be constantly aware of these attacks, able to identify them.

What antidote did Paul prescribe for the malignant heresy in the church? Preach the Word. On the heels of his exhortation to "continue in the things you have learned"[121] and his encouragement of the profitability and adequacy of the Scripture for every good work, Paul reiterated Timothy's divine responsibility to teach God's Word for the Spiritual well-being of the church.

Many homes are outfitted with the required fire alarms in

living spaces to be compliant with safety standards. However, often fire alarms are ignored because they can be falsely triggered by cooking accidents such as crumbs left in the toaster. Perhaps more crucial than these alarms, are the carbon monoxide alarms that safety experts recommend. These devices detect the odorless, colorless gas that is extremely deadly. Carbon monoxide is dangerous because people can breathe the gas completely unaware that they are slowly suffocating. They need the shrill of the alarm to alert them to the danger.

In the Christian life, scriptural literacy and biblically-sound preaching serves as our carbon monoxide alarm. Paul warned against those who look for new teachers as sources of entertainment, calling it "ear tickling." In today's current age of limitless streaming and glut of information, Christians can easily fall into this trap, even for the wiles of false teachers who, "by their smooth and flattering speech they deceive the hearts of the unsuspecting" (Romans 16:18b).

These smooth talkers can be subtle. Perhaps for some, the trap is a motivational teacher who calls themselves a Christian. One might listen without discernment, unguarded due to their assumption that the speaker holds to orthodox teaching. This can be a Christian professor at a Christian school offering decisively anti-Christian advice. It can be a pastor at the pulpit of your church who has slowly compromised his theology, and now pays homage to the culture and the feelings of his community.

How do you respond to Timothy's charge to preach the Word? We respond by taking seriously the urgent call to be grounded in God's Word. The need for scriptural literacy is as dire now as in Paul's day. Our children deserve mothers who are grounded, steadfast and unshaken by the trending religious movements.

We also must become prayer warriors for the faithful men that serve in our communities, sharing God's Word. Their dedication to scriptural integrity is essential. We must support them, pray for them, and listen *with prudence* to the words they preach. When we have faithful teachers, we should praise God, and communicate our gratitude to them for their diligent study.

False teachers will always malign our faith. Don't panic. Keep focused on the Word of God. Teach your children the Word of God. It is always our defense.

How might you preach the Word in your circle of influence?

_____

_____

_____

_____

_____

_____

TWENTY THREE

CHANGING OF THE GUARD

For I am already being poured out as a drink offering, and the time of my departure has come. I have fought the good fight, I have finished the course, I have kept the faith; in the future there is laid up for me the crown of righteousness, which the Lord, the righteous Judge, will award to me on that day; and not only to me, but also to all who have loved His appearing.

2 TIMOTHY 4:6-8

FROM ONE'S DEATHBED, TRUE character is exposed. In the final minutes of life, some wallow in self-pity while others hurriedly offer apologies decades overdue. One godly woman in my circle of friends offered a simple phrase as her physical body was overcome to the rages of cancer: "No turning back." She was committed fully to her Lord and Savior, and her final physical suffering would do nothing to sway her from her commitment to Christ.

Paul offered a similar living epitaph in his closing thoughts to Timothy. From the confines of his Roman prison, he attested to a faithful life. He was confident that he had fulfilled his calling with obedience, that he would finish his life with excellence, and that in his future home, he would be generously recompensed. He was satisfied, content, and filled with hope.

Paul had taken honest stock of his circumstances, and reconciled that all that remained for him on earth was death. Scholar John MacArthur clarified, "Because Roman citizens could not be crucified, he knew that he likely would be beheaded, literally pouring out his own blood for the Lord."[122] Both Greek and Jewish believers were well-acquainted with the ritual of animal sacrifice, from where this verbiage originated. For this specific religious gift, Jewish priests would prepare a combination of oil and wine, often as an addition to a blood sacrifice as a peace offering or in conjunction with a religious festival. The ritual mixture offset the pungent odor of the blood of the animal, giving a pleasing aroma in the sacrifice. Elsewhere, Paul wrote, "For to me, to live is Christ and to die is gain,"[123] a testimony that he saw his life and death as a vehicle for worship.

Paul's verbiage revealed his Christ-focused attitude. He had suffered greatly as a Christian, but when facing his final earthly trial, there was no despair that marked his tone. He saw his death as a final act of obedience to the Lord, and anticipated the heavenly rewards he knew he would soon enjoy.

Paul's confident anticipation of death was a combination of obedient service and joy-filled expectation. Paul had no regrets. Many years before, he shared his testimony. "Brethren, I have lived my life with a perfectly good conscience before God up to this day" (Acts 23:1b). Despite his failures before Christ—being a persecutor of the church, and his previous spiritual blindness and pride—Paul knew that he had been forgiven. In Christ, he was offered a chance to start over, and he had been faithful to the calling that forgiveness had placed on him.

Paul had confidence not only in his justification before God, but in the glorious future he had in Christ. With the throng of other faithful believers, he anticipated worshipping his Savior eternally, and dwelling forever in His presence. He clung to this hope without tears, mourning, crying, or pain.[124] He also knew that the work he had done was to be rewarded by Jesus Christ Himself. In an act of supreme submission and expectant hope, Paul placed his past and future in the hands of his Savior, and looked to Timothy to carry on his work.

There is a demeanor of patient hope and quiet rest that characterizes those fully reliant upon the person of God. In this complete reliance, there is peace, despite present circumstances or future outcomes. Paul existed in this place, unshaken by the torrents of difficulty he faced. With this composure, he was able to pass the baton from his aging, weathered hand to the younger hand of Timothy. Not only would the Lord accomplish His purposes for Paul, but for Timothy and for the church at large. There was no pretense; no last-minute need for recognition. Just the simple realization that his successor would continue to run the race.

The planet needs more people like Paul. In a world where emotionalism and reactiveness govern decisions, Paul's steady gaze on Christ offers a silent challenge. Do we trust Christ in this way? As we raise our children and prepare them to go into a dark world, do we look around, wild-eyed and panicked, or do we keep our focus on faithfully completing the mission Christ has for us?

Nothing should keep us from being faithful to our Master. God might be calling some mamas who read this to a hard road of discipleship. Perhaps this road involves a debilitating or terminal illness. Maybe we are called to raise our children in the midst of financial insecurity or family instability. We will do well to model the lifestyle of Paul, understanding that our earthly mission is to fight the good fight, to finish the course, to keep the faith.

This means we put one foot in front of the other, and be faithful with the very next thing—the next Christ-honoring response; the next task done well; the next answer in love. We do this while keeping in mind that everything we do is an act of worship, and a testimony of our faith in Christ. If we trust our good God, we need never be hurried or anxious. We are secure in Him, able to withstand the worst of life's blows, confidently looking forward to the future which He has prepared for us and our children.

What is the next right thing that God has called you to do?

_____

_____

_____

_____

TWENTY FOUR

A TIME TO COMFORT

*Make every effort to come to me soon; for Demas,
having loved this present world, has deserted
me and gone to Thessalonica; Crescens has
gone to Galatia, Titus to Dalmatia. Only Luke is with
me. Pick up Mark and bring him with you, for he
is useful to me for service. But Tychicus I have sent
to Ephesus. When you come bring the cloak which I
left at Troas with Carpus, and the books, especially
the parchments. Alexander the coppersmith
did me much harm; the Lord will repay him
according to his deeds. Be on guard against him
yourself, for he vigorously opposed our teaching.*

2 TIMOTHY 4:9-15

IT IS SAID THAT you can boil a frog alive because it will
not immediately notice the discomfort. Slowly, incrementally,
the rising temperature will cook the animal before it realizes
the need to respond. For some people, suffering is like that.
It creeps upon them until it becomes difficult to bear. Paul's
suffering was at a rolling boil. There was no attempt to escape.
His fate seemed sealed.

In this chapter's Scripture, the seriousness of Paul's physical situation is revealed. Though he offers a Christ-focused message in 2 Timothy, the final verses lend clarity to the depth of the apostle's personal pain. Paul had suffered before and experienced lows in his life, but everything that came previously seemed to pale in the shadow of his final trial. With few friends to lift the burden of isolation, Paul was virtually alone. He had been deserted and betrayed by some of the friends nearest to him. His days of influence were over. In his last days, Paul was poor, neglected, dirty, kept with criminals, and awaiting execution. What an end for a faithful servant of God.

These verses were not an idle complaint, however. There were two reasons for Paul to share his rejection. He had already written about the body of Christ, and the need for its parts to function in unison. He explained that the body suffered together and rejoiced together, and here he was in desperate need of Timothy to suffer with him.[125]

Paul was honest about the difficulties he was facing, and also mentioned specific ways in which Timothy could help him. He was humble, and eager to receive the help of a brother in Christ. Paul was also offering a kind of final State of the Union address, illuminating concerns in the life of the church that would no doubt involve Timothy. John MacArthur puts it this way:

> "Paul did not write this section as an afterthought; it was not incidental but vital to the Spirit-inspired message. The Lord wanted the rest of His church to know about these people in Paul's life and to learn from their faithfulness or their failure."[126]

These were names that Paul knew Timothy was familiar with. Men who had claimed the name of Christ, and advanced His Kingdom. Men who had caused deep pain to the apostle, and could still cause continued damage. These were people that Paul and Timothy had worked alongside and shared life with, only to have them turn aside from the faith. Paul mentioned two men, Demas and Alexander, who had both caused deep hurt for the early church. Demas made multiple appearances in the Pauline epistles, and seemed to be a close associate of Paul and Timothy.

Whether Demas' vice was human comfort or fear of oppression, the self-denial required of Christ-followers caused him to turn aside from his faith. Scholars suggest that Demas' departure for Thessalonica was an opportunity to flee persecution, and perhaps even return to an unsaved lifestyle.[127]

The name Alexander is referenced multiple times in the New Testament, but this man is not clearly linked with any of the other appearances. While the exact harm he caused Paul isn't clearly stated, it seems likely that he either spread false doctrine or was involved in Paul's arrest. As a leader in the church, Timothy needed this painful intel to insightfully protect his flock against attack.

Even in his last days, Paul was the consummate missionary. Of his few remaining friends, Paul had sent several away to continue Gospel work. These he outlined clearly along with the locations, likely so Timothy could follow up with them after his death. In Paul's requests for help, he referenced a desire to have Mark join him again in ministry. These two had a sorted past. Many years before, Paul had discouraged Mark in a missionary journey, but this seemed to be long since amended. Paul wanted to finish his life unified with his brothers, and actively serving the Lord.

Nestled between his warnings and missions' updates was a glimpse into his personal needs. Paul was physically cold. After a stint in a Roman prison, Paul's clothing was surely in tatters, and he needed the cloak for warmth and some sense of privacy in the crowded jail. He also longed for his books, a last pleasure and connection with his old life. The parchments were likely Scripture, and in these dark days, Paul desperately needed the comfort of God's Word.

It seems almost pathetic that a hero of the faith would be reduced to these meager requests—things that we easily take for granted. But this great man had learned the fundamental lesson of contentment. And while he would not grovel or complain, he desired his last days to be wholly focused on the Lord, and the warmth and spiritual writings would aid him in this, his final stretch of the race.

Separated by two millennia, we would do well to learn from the Apostle Paul as he took stock of his surroundings before his death. He shared truth with Timothy, but he steered away from gossip. He didn't delve into the failings of Demas or Alexander, nor did he commend himself for the sacrifice of commissioning Tychicus, or losing Crescens and Titus for Gospel work. He didn't feign independence, either. He asked for help from trusted friends who he could depend upon.

In our day, the church is filled with people who have real, tangible needs. Simple needs, like friendship and fellowship that Christians are able to fill. Unfortunately, often we are too proud to ask for help, and too busy to notice a need. But in the pews of our churches, and perhaps on the sofa in our homes, men, women, and children are desperate for the comfort and encouragement of the body of Christ.

In light of that fact, we can become the hands and feet of Jesus when we seek out these needs then work diligently to fill them. This begins with something as simple as inviting a family over for dinner, or sitting across the table from your teen to have an unhurried conversation. We become aware of our codependency upon the body of Christ when we search out the needs of our spiritual family, and work to meet them. This requires time, attention, and care.

More than just having a girls' night with your best friends, and a passing, "How are you doing?" as you walk your church hallways. It takes seeing a friend hurting, then committing to pray for them. It takes delving into Scripture with them, or caring for their children so they can go on a date with their spouse. It takes intentionality and possibly a little bit of awkwardness, getting involved in the lives of others.

Sadly, this is an idea foreign to our world today. We live frenzied and overcommitted, unable to see past the colored blocks in our Google calendars. But we demonstrate the transformational love of Christ to a lost and hurting world when we meet the needs of our Christian family in the name of Jesus. We also show our reliance upon Christ when we expose our needs to those in our orbit, and allow them to comfort us when we are in need. This begins within our own four walls, with our own families.

Do our children have needs we don't see? Find them, meet them. Treat them with the mercy and compassion of Jesus.

Are you ready to be someone's lifeline? Who is in need of you right now?

_____

_____

_____

_____

_____

_____

_____

_____

_____

TWENTY FIVE

THE SUSTAINING POWER OF CHRIST

At my first defense no one supported me, but all deserted me; may it not be counted against them. But the Lord stood with me and strengthened me, so that through me the proclamation might be fully accomplished, and that all the Gentiles might hear; and I was rescued out of the lion's mouth. The Lord will rescue me from every evil deed, and will bring me safely to His heavenly kingdom; to Him be the glory forever and ever. Amen.

2 TIMOTHY 4:16-18

THERE WAS A SEASON not long ago when a pandemic severely damaged interpersonal relationships. This unprecedented health crisis forced medical professionals to respond with minimal data while trying their best to keep casualties contained. Among the immunocompromised and the elderly, isolation was encouraged. The world quickly became estranged from itself as people were told not to attend church or gather with friends or loved ones.

Among the most impacted were nursing home residents, kept in their rooms for long months, devoid of interaction and friendship. For many, the cognitive decline they experienced during their isolation was devastating. Unlike ever before, this global crisis underscored the necessity for people living in community.

The Apostle Paul used some of the last few verses in 2 Timothy to share the depth of his isolation in his final days. He said that in his trial, he was there alone. Scholars comment on why things turned out this way for Paul. Surely there was a reason for Onesiphorus and Luke not being at the trial, as they did not seem deterred by guilt by association. But likely, the absence of any Roman or Jewish believer was motivated by fear. Due to the prominence of Paul as a religious figure and the spoken appeal he had made to Ceasar, it is reasonable to assume that Nero himself presided over his case.[128] Perhaps the name alone struck sufficient fear to cause Paul's friends to flee.

This evil ruler had been responsible for the mass execution of Christians in the most savage and barbaric means imaginable. Nero was famed for his erratic behavior and volatile temper. Christians had every earthly reason to fear. Yet, the church's betrayal of Paul in his moment of greatest need proved an opportunity for Christ to sustain him in a way only He could.

Charles Spurgeon writes of this sort of dependence on Christ in articulate detail:

> "Some of you know what it is to be deserted by
> your friends in the hour of your greatest need...
> Oh, but we never fully know Christ until such

a time as that! We never realize the sweetness
of His sympathetic companionship until He
stands by us and we can say with Paul, 'At
my first defense, no one came to my aid, but
all deserted me. But the Lord helped me and
strengthened me.'"[129]

Before he was called by Christ, Paul had possessed everything. He had fame and wealth, position and the favor of the
crowd. From an earthly perspective, knowing Christ had cost
Paul everything. Yet, in His place of supreme weakness, Paul
experienced the sustaining power of Christ, as he leaned on
His strength like never before.

Jesus had promised circumstances like these during His
earthly ministry. He had promised difficulty and persecution
and judgement. But He also promised God's intervention in
those moments, giving the right words at the right time.[130] And
before His ascension to the Father, Jesus had promised His
presence would be with believers until the end of the age.[131]
Now Paul attested to Christ's veracity to His promise. Christ
had stood by him. And although Paul was forgotten by his
friends, Jesus sustained him through to the end.

Paul said that he was delivered from the lion's mouth,
which was synonymous for mortal danger, but might also have
been brutally literal. Nero condemned prisoners to be mauled
by wild animals, and for some reason, Paul was spared this
fate. Perhaps so he could write this final letter.

Paul wrote with confidence that God would rescue him
from every evil deed, and safely bring him into His heavenly
kingdom. He wrote these words as a condemned criminal, but
he wasn't a victim, but a victor. He anticipated God's grace to

bring him through whatever violent end would finally release him from prison. He knew that whatever came, it would be worth it. God would richly reward him.

Paul wrote with conviction in the midst of crushing circumstances. He passed the test, but the brothers and sisters who should have been his closest allies and prayer warriors, failed miserably. Scripture gives clear direction that believers are to empathize and care for those suffering for the cause of Christ. The writer of Hebrews reminds believers, "Remember the prisoners, as though in prison with them, *and* those who are ill-treated, since you yourselves also are in the body" (Matthew 10:19b).

Missions agencies go to great lengths to highlight the plight of Christians in closed or hostile countries. But the stories of modern-day heroes that suffer and lose their lives for the Gospel are difficult to digest. And even harder to step into. In this day and culture of isolationism and apathy, it is all too easy to let believers struggle alone. It is simpler to allow pastors and ministry staff to do the bulk of the heavy lifting. But the difficulties faced by our brothers and sisters aren't someone else's problem. Scripture tells us that our witness as believers is in our love. "By this all men will know that you are My disciples, if you have love for one another" (John 13:35).

This begins within our homes. We mother in a world gone wrong by showing our children love done right. We mother our children with love and compassion, seeking to meet their deepest needs, and be the hands and feet of Christ in crisis. It is a consuming task—ongoing from birth long into adulthood—as we learn to shepherd and guide our children throughout the many seasons of their lives. Of this task, theologian and author Tedd Tripp writes, "The task God has given you is not one that can be conveniently scheduled. It is a pervasive task. Training and shepherding are going on wherever you are with your children."[132]

Our children see us live out our faith in our interactions with them and others. We model Christ-like sacrificial love by meeting the needs of the people around us. We can do this by reaching out to the old woman from your church suffering from chronic pain. We show Christ's love by wading into her misery, by checking in on her, and pointing her to Scripture. This is a need so often ignored. People need hope, and what better resource than God's love letter.

The writer of Psalm 119:25 points to the sustaining power of Scripture: "My soul cleaves to the dust; Revive me according to Your word."

People need to be encouraged with the Word of God, and pointed to the truth that can offer lasting hope. We need to be reminded of the promises of God. Another Psalm adds, "I would have despaired unless I had believed that I would see the goodness of the Lord In the land of the living" (Psalm 27:13). Though there are multiple contributors to the Book of Psalms, each chapter and verse ring with the same divinity, sovereignty, and inspiration.

God is faithful to sustain His followers, even in the worst of circumstances. Paul testified to that truth, even when he hit his lowest point. Christ stood by him and held him up. God did that in a space where all the Christians around Paul had abandon him. But God's faithfulness didn't.

God is able to sustain His church, and to bring each believer safely into His kingdom. We are wise to gratefully anticipate this heavenly homecoming. As we walk alongside a hurting brother or browbeaten sister, we are lifting the darkness in our corner of the world. We are advancing the Gospel's mission, and doing our part to see the Lord's kingdom come, participating in the miraculous sustaining power of Christ.

In what ways do your children see a mother that loves well? What special gifts do you bring?

_____

_____

_____

_____

_____

_____

_____

TWENTY SIX

IN THE END

Greet Prisca and Aquila, and the household
of Onesiphorus. Erastus remained at Corinth,
but Trophimus I left sick at Miletus. Make every effort
to come before winter. Eubulus greets you, also
Pudens and Linus and Claudia and all the brethren.
The Lord be with your spirit. Grace be with you.

2 TIMOTHY 4:19-22

IN A LIFE LIVED solely for Jesus, few words need to be spoken at the end. There are no burned bridges to repair, for submission to Jesus requires accounts kept short. There is no final flurry of advice or agony of what-ifs. A life of submission to Christ produces a death permeated with deep satisfaction—joyfully expectant of the life to come rather than desperately attached to the one that is passing.

This is the essence of Paul's final words to Timothy. Greetings from friends. A desire for fellowship. A benediction for the Lord's presence to guard him. It is humble and simple and beautiful. This closing seems almost casual for the goodbye of dear cohorts after almost two decades of side-by-side service. And yet the lack of grasping or groping for comfort shows the heart of an apostle. Paul embraced the process of leaving, and he was ready. There was little left to be said other than declaring his love for the brethren and his confidence in Christ. Little else mattered.

Some things never change. It is too easy to get caught up in today's business that provides little time to consider the things God has given us—the things that really matter in the end. Our relationship with Christ. Family. Friends. Community. We are often so discouraged by the world around us, that we're overwhelmed by fear, worries, and our exhausting schedule. We miss the importance of what God has given us right now.

Paul took time to reflect on this goodness of God in the simple gifts of fellowship, friendship, and faith. He passed along greetings to his old ministry and business partners whom he had served in tent-making during his early missionary days. He shared the needs of believers, though Scripture says little on that topic. Surely Timothy knew them, and would reach out to them personally.

Paul shared the greetings of people mentioned nowhere else in Scripture—people with Greek names and unknown backgrounds, silent testimonies to the growth and vibrancy of the church. From prison in Rome, Paul saw the church growing. His time was coming to an end, but he knew this wasn't the end—not for the Church of Jesus Christ.

Pudens, Linus and Claudia, Luke and Timothy, (you and I) would carry the Good News of Jesus into the final days of Jesus' return, eradicating evil and bringing peace to the earth. But until that day came, Paul was just a man needing strength to face the executioner's block.

History does not provide a specific date, but church tradition shares that some short time after Paul asked God's grace to be upon Timothy, he relied upon that grace for himself. And when his day came, he was brought out of his cell and led to a place of execution—along the Ostrian Way outside of Rome. As the solider commissioned with ending the life of this holy man, separating his head from his body, Paul's mission was done. Now, he was *absent from the body, present with the Lord*. His reward had begun. The hopes and dreams of decades were realized as he met his Savior face-to-face. His life of suffering for the Cross was a small price to pay.

He left behind almost no possessions. A few scrolls and a cloak. This great apostle had lost everything, except for Christ. He left this world penniless, counting it all as rubbish. He was mourned and missed by friends, most of all by Timothy, his long-term protégé. But with Paul's death, Timothy's time to step up and run the race was now before him.

In retrospect, did Timothy do all that God had planned for him? Did he heed the words of his mentor, and weather the difficulty of the times, being consistent and faithful to the Lord? We can only imagine he did, as tradition states that he later died a martyr's death as well. But Paul couldn't know that. In the end, all Paul could do was entrust is beloved spiritual son to the grace of God to sustain him.

In the end, that's really all any of us can do. We raise our children with our eyes on Christ, and our hands open to faithful to teach, instruct, and remind them over and over of the things they have been taught. What Truth really is. At the end of the day, raising children in an evil world means entrusting the Lord to protect their spirit. It means a life full of faithful service, and joy-filled rest as we depend completely on the Lord to bring about a good outcome for our children for His glory.

Because His glory is where all good is found.

Final Thought

Can you relate to the Apostle Paul? Do you see yourself in the midst of this deeply personal letter to Timothy? Likely not. Hopefully not. But we can come into a deeper understanding of the faithfulness of God who saved a self-righteous Pharisee and turned him into a devoted Christ-follower. We see the testimony of a changed life, and the promise of God's sustaining power to protect His church until His second coming. And so as we wait for that day in a world that is so opposed to His truth. We raise our children in the best way we can—in faith and adherence to the Word of God. If our children are already grown, we mother them from a distance the best we can, pointing them to God's Word and loving them with His love.

The climate changes. Our settings may shift. We might not always relate to each other. But the mandate for Christ-honoring mamas remains the same throughout time.

Guard, through the Holy Spirit who dwells in us,
the treasure which has been entrusted to you.

2 TIMOTHY 1:14

STUDY
GUIDE QUESTIONS

Session 1: Introduction, Chapters 1-2

1. (Warm-up) If you knew that you were coming to the end of your life, what types of things would you want to tell your children, or someone else who would come after you?

2. **Read II Timothy 1:1-4.** Even though Paul is not a mother, we will be looking to learn from him as he instructs his spiritual son, Timothy. What were Paul's circumstances as he was writing this letter?

3. Why is it important to know the background before starting a book like II Timothy?

4. What was Paul's specific mission as an apostle and how did he receive this assignment?

5. How did Paul regard Timothy? What type of a relationship did they have?

6. What type of advice and counsel would you expect a person like Paul will give a beloved son like Timothy?

7. Surprisingly, Paul begins by praying for Timothy with gratefulness. Why is it important to cultivate gratefulness in our roles as mothers?

8. Paul prays for Timothy constantly and affectionately. What are some ways that you have found helpful in making prayer a more practical part of your day?

9. For this week: As we start this study of II Timothy, consider the people around you that God has entrusted you with, whether your own children or others in your life over whom you have influence. Consider keeping a list of things you are grateful for about these dear ones to share with our group at the next meeting. Take a moment now and pray for each of them by name.

Session 2: Chapters 3-4

1. (Warm-up) Would anyone like to share something you are grateful about one of the people in your life? Or perhaps something that was said or done this week that you are grateful for?

2. **Read II Timothy 1:1-7.** What challenges you most about your stage of mothering? (If you don't have children of your own, think about your interactions with those you are trying to influence or mentor)

3. How did Timothy's heritage of a godly mother and grandmother benefit or influence him?

4. Can you think of any examples of how godly heritage has influenced you? Share one with the group. How can you imitate that example in your mothering?

5. What are some of the habits you learned from your mother or grandmother that you want to pass along to those who follow after you?

6. When we are facing tough times, as Paul and Timothy

were, how does a word of encouragement make a difference?

7. For this week: What are some areas of your mothering where you could benefit from encouragement? Look around your group. Take a few minutes to offer words of sincere encouragement to those in your group today. Consider reaching out to one of the members of your group during the week to encourage her in her calling as a mother.

Session 3: Chapters 5-6

1. (Warm-up) Did you have anything good happen in your mothering adventures that you would like to share this week? Any small wins?

2. **Read II Timothy 1:8-12.** In this day and age, what are some areas which require courage for mothers? What are some ways that we might experience suffering as mothers?

3. Paul calls Timothy to live as a Christ-follower, realizing that his calling was worth it. Think about your own life. What are some of the things that God has called you to do right now.

4. What is one practical way you can demonstrate Christ in your specific calling today?

5. In our world, there is a lot of relativism. What are some things which we know to be absolutes?

6. How does knowing Christ and his character help us to gain confidence in our calling?

7. Paul asserts that God holds the future. How does this knowledge add to our courage and confidence in facing that future?

8. For this week: Take a moment to write II Timothy 1:12b and place it somewhere where you are likely to see it. Think about the areas of your mothering where you lack confidence. During this week when you are tempted to worry about this, try turning this over to God using II Timothy 1:12b.

Session 4: Chapters 7-8

1. (Warm-up) Did any of you use II Timothy 1:12b to counter difficult times or curb worry this last week? Would anyone like to share their experience?

2. **Read II Timothy 1:13-18**. What are some areas in life where it is absolutely essential to follow directions or patterns? What are some of the outcomes if these are ignored?

3. What can we do as mothers to be sure that we are competent "pattern followers"?

4. How is this type of "victorious living" different from the idea of being "supermoms"?

5. Moms are to practically and diligently guard those under her care in her house. What are some of the ways we do this physically? How can we do this spiritually?

6. Why is it important to guard our mouths as mothers?

7. Paul mentions the encouraging influence of Onesiphorus in his life, telling of how he refreshed

him while he had been incarcerated. Can you think of anyone who has ever refreshed you as you have struggled in your season of mothering?

8. Grace is necessary when dealing with the people around us, be they husbands, children, or workmates. How does recognizing that you have received grace from God help you to extend grace to those around you?

9. Think again of someone who has refreshed you or shown you grace at a time when you really needed it. Have you ever thanked that person? Consider taking five minutes to write a brief note of thanks to one person who has refreshed you or shown you extra grace.

Session 5: Chapters 9-10

1. (Warm-up) Did any of you think of someone to write to last week? Did anyone do it? Can you share anything about that person and why you wrote to thank them?

2. **Read II Timothy 2:1-2.** Who is the strongest person (physically speaking) that you know? Who is the strongest person you know in some other way? Why do you consider this person to be strong?

3. What are some ways in which God calls us to be strong?

4. What does it mean to be strong in mind? How can we cultivate this in our children?

5. Why is it important to be strong in our convictions?

6. What are some reasons we are not strong? What are some ways we can change these?

7. Repetition is so important to pass our faith to the next generation. Have you found any clever ways to use repetition in teaching your children about the Word and their faith?

8. We have an awesome task as mothers and all of us can use some strengthening. Challenge yourself this week. How about repeating and memorizing II Timothy 2:2 to remind yourself of your calling and the task in front of you. Write it down; put it where you can see it; carry it around; repeat it to yourself several times a day. Let's try a little strengthening of our spiritual muscles! (The things which you have heard from me in the presence of many witnesses, entrust these to faithful men who will be able to teach others also. 2 Timothy 2:2)

Session 6: Chapters 11-12

1. Let's try to see if we can say our verse from last week. How did it go? Did the repetition help? How did this verse challenge you in your mothering this week?

2. **Read II Timothy 2:3-13**. Have any of you ever trained for a race? (or known someone who did) What sorts of things does a runner do to prepare for an important race?

3. How do soldiers and farmers show similar dedication?

4. In what areas of mothering is dedication and discipline important? What are possible results if a mother chooses to be undisciplined and undedicated to her task?

5. What rewards do we see for this type of dedication in this life? In the life to come?

6. What circumstances in your life can cause you the most discouragement? What do you usually do when you are discouraged?

7. Paul was in very difficult circumstances as he wrote this letter. What were some of those circumstances? How did he keep from being discouraged?

8. How do his affirmation statements in v. 11-13 help him to regain his courage in the face of such difficult circumstances?

9. What is one area you have experienced discouragement in your mothering in the last week? Take a moment and pray, inviting the Holy Spirit to encourage your heart with the truths of His strength to accomplish your task. Use the statements in v. 11-13 in your prayer, praying them back to God to help you recognize His faithfulness in helping and strengthening you. When you are tempted to be discouraged this week, take a moment and pray for God's help, acknowledging that "He remains faithful."

Session 7: Chapters 13-14

1. (Warm-up) Last week we were encouraged to pray and ask for God's faithful help when we were discouraged. Did any of you try that? How did it go?

2. **Read II Timothy 2:14-19.** Can you think of any time when empty or wrong words about another person or persons severed relationships? This is a common theme in books or movies; someone overhears part of what is said, or misunderstands, and relationships are

jeopardized until the closing ten minutes or the last ten pages. Why are words so important?

3. What kinds of sins can we commit with words? Why are these easy to commit?

4. What can we do to try to combat these types of struggles in ourselves? Can you think of any Scripture which can help us in our battle against this sin?

5. Since sins of the mouth are so easy to commit, how can we bring them to a halt?

6. When we struggle in our battle with sin, how does knowing we are "sealed in Christ" offer us hope and encouragement?

7. Paul says that "everyone who names the name of the Lord is to abstain from wickedness." Considering that, what answer would you give to someone who would say that "no one is perfect"?

8. This is a hard application this week! Let's think about cleaning up our mouths. You know where your biggest area of struggle is with your mouth. Take a moment and confess that to the Lord. This week, let's begin each day committing to abstaining from evil on our tongues!

Session 8: Chapters 15-16

1. (Warm-up) How did it go with your tongue this week? Did anyone have any victories in this area?

2. **Read II Timothy 2:20-26**. Can you think of something you took out of your home or moved out of reach when

you had little people in your home (maybe you still do!)? What might have happened if you had left it where they could reach it?

3. God wants us to serve Him in the right manner and with the right motives. What are some wrong motives that some may have while appearing to serve the Lord?

4. How can diligently knowing God's Word keep us from these wrong motives?

5. Why is it especially important that church leaders guard their speech?

6. How about mothers–why should we be especially careful to guard what we say?

7. What are some areas that mothers are prone to slip with their tongues? Think about this last week, as we focused on the tongue last week. When did you find it the hardest to guard your tongue? What helped you to curb it?

8. This week, let's focus on this verse: "Set a guard, O LORD, over my mouth; Keep watch over the door of my lips." (Psalm 141:3) Envision the Lord as setting a literal guard over your mouth. Ask Him to check what goes out for his standards! Consider googling and printing a picture of a Roman guard and imagine a little guard like that over your mouth. (Leaders–maybe you can bring little pictures of this!) Bring this little guard with you this week to remind yourselves to "set a guard."

Session 9: Chapters 17-18

1. (Warm-up) Did any of you use the guard last week? Do any of you have your "guard" with you? Did this visual reminder help you in guarding your speech?

2. **Read II Timothy 3:1-9.** This section begins with the phrase, "In the last days difficult times will come." In what ways are believers today experiencing difficult times?

3. Why does Paul take so much time describing these people who want nothing to do with God?

4. How can we identify people who hold to a form of godliness in our churches? What should we do about these people? Why should we pay attention to whether or not they are around us?

5. How can we train our children to be alert to these "false believers" or "wolves"?

6. How can we defend Paul in this passage for calling some women "silly women"? Why did he label them as such?

7. What are some of the dangerous results of being a foolish woman (according to the Proverbs)?

8. What things seem to predispose some women to fall into the traps of wrong teaching more than others?

9. What safeguards can we use to be sure that we are not falling for false teachers?

10. Take a few moments this week to evaluate what teachers you are listening to and what books you are reading.

Carefully weigh what you hear and read. Does it line up with Scripture? If you are unsure, ask a trusted older believer to give it a second look for you. This week, consider forgoing one of your favorite podcasts to spend that extra time listening to the Bible online. Take it with you to the gym, on a walk, or listen to it in the kitchen as you cook or as you clean up or fold laundry. See what a difference infusing the Scripture into your day can make this week.

Session 10: Chapters 19-20

1. (Warm-up) Did any of you try taking the Scripture with you as you were in your daily routine? Did you see any difference or learn anything new?

2. **Read II Timothy 3:10-15** (Leader: consider bringing a book with stories of modern day Christians who have undergone difficulties to share with the group. One such book is When Faith Is Forbidden). If not available, use this question: Can you think of anyone in modern times who has suffered or been persecuted for Christ's sake? Why did they do this? What was the result for them?

3. Why did Paul share this part of his experience? What was he hoping to accomplish?

4. What evidence of God's faithfulness have you seen in your life or in the lives of those close to you? Can you think of something specific to share with the group?

5. Paul exhorts Timothy to "remain" in what he has learned and been taught. Can you think of something

that you were taught as a child (good or bad) that "remains" with you until today?

6. For you who were raised in a Christian home, can you think of the first verse you learned in your home?

7. What would you say to those who say that teaching Scripture to young children is too hard for them to understand?

8. What is the value in teaching very young children to memorize verses of Scripture?

9. Here is a challenge for you this week! If you have any children in your home, try learning a verse of Scripture with them this week. Possibly consider II Timothy 3:14, or maybe another verse you want to imprint on the minds in your household. Introduce this verse tonight or tomorrow and say it with your children every day the next week. Let's see what happens! (If you don't have children, or they are too young to talk, try this anyway, saying this verse to yourself at the same time every day. Let's learn Scripture!)

Session 11: Chapters 21-22

1. (Warm-up) Did you memorize with your kids this week? What verse did you learn? Were they better at memorizing than you were? Did you think about this verse during the day? Did it make any difference?

2. **Read II Timothy 3:16-4:5.** When you have a moment to spend reading the Scriptures, where do you tend to go? What are some of your favorites? What are some areas of Scripture that you wish you knew more about or want to study?

3. This familiar verse asserts that "All Scripture is inspired by God." What does this mean, as the Scripture is a compilation of many books written across a vast period of time?

4. The verse goes on to claim that "all Scripture....is profitable..." Are there sections of Scripture that you struggle to understand how they are profitable? Share some of these with the group. How do we handle the harder parts of Scripture?

5. We are all in different seasons of our lives, where the study of the Scripture looks different for each of us. How would you describe the season of your study? What can you do to guard your time in the Word in the season you are in. Share some of the things that have worked for you.

6. In the final section for today, Paul exhorts Timothy to "preach the Word." Since none of us is a preacher by profession, how do we "preach" in our everyday lives?

7. Paul's motivation for his urgency is the fact of his approaching death. What motivations do we have for sharing this important message with our children and those around us?

8. Why is being spiritually literate essential to complete the command to "preach the Word"?

9. Think of our opening exercise where you were asked to think about an area of Scripture you wish you knew more about. Decide to take a step toward changing that this week. Read part or all of this section during the week. Look toward a trusted Bible teacher and listen

to a sermon on this part of Scripture. Talk to an older Christian to get insight where you have questions. Let's use this week to grow!

Session 12: Chapters 23-24

10. (Warm-up) Did you explore a new section of Scripture this week? What were some of the sections you studied or explored? Did you learn something new or unexpected?

11. **Read II Timothy 4:6-15**. When you think about Heaven, what do you believe it will be like? What are some things you are looking forward to? What are some things you have questions about?

12. As you think about your life, what are some things that you hope people will remember and say about you?

13. What are some things you would like your children to say about you?

14. If you knew you only had a specific length of time left, what would you try to say or teach to your children?

15. Paul asked for help in these last sections. In our society, we often exalt self-sufficiency, but why is it important to also learn to ask for help?

16. How can you discern the needs of those people around you? What are some examples of needs we can meet around us? If you have children, how can you have your children participate in meeting these needs?

17. This week, seek to meet someone's practical need, preferably involve your children too! Consider sharing

a meal or taking a meal to someone, visiting an older person in a nursing home, calling a lonely friend on the phone, writing notes to someone...the list is endless. If you have a need in your life, don't hide! Look for an older, godly woman with whom you can share your heart, and least pray together. Let's give the body of Christ a chance to serve this week!

Session 13: Chapters 25-26

1. (Warm-up) Did you meet someone's needs this week? Does anyone want to share an experience of meeting needs?

2. **Read II Timothy 4:16-22.** Have you ever had an experience in which you felt (and perhaps were) completely alone? How did you feel in that isolating time?

3. Who are some people or professions that you can think of where people might tend to feel alone? How can mothers sometimes feel alone in their tasks?

4. How can we help to alleviate some of these feelings of "aloneness" or isolation in the people or professions we have mentioned?

5. As a mother, how can you take steps to eliminate your own feelings of isolation? What are some things we can do to counteract these feelings?

6. How does fellowship help to deal with feelings of isolation and depression? Where can you find fellowship like this?

7. As you travel down your mothering journey, reflect on what you have learned. What priorities are most

important in your journey? What are some of the most important things you can do with/for your children at this point in your mothering journey.

8. Final challenge: If you have physical children who are out of your home, consider writing them each a letter in the next week. Encourage them and tell them how you are praying for them. If you have children in the home, consider writing a letter for them for a later point in their lives (18th birthday, after college....your choice), and tell them how you are praying for them now. If you don't have children, choose a younger person in your church or small group and write a letter telling them how you are praying for them. Let's leave a legacy of prayer, encouragement and godly living!

NOTES

1   "The Story Behind the Famous Kiss", By Lawrence Verria and Captain George Galdorisi, U.S. Navy (Retired) July 2012 Naval History Magazine, Volume 26, Number 4. https://www.usni. org/magazines/naval-history-magazine/2012/july/story-behind-famous-kiss

2   Matthew 3:17

3   Agapētos, *Strong's Greek Lexicon*, Entry G27.

4   1 Timothy 1:2

5   Acts 16

6   Eirēnē- *Strong's Greek Lexicon*, Entry G1515.

7   John MacArthur, The MacArthur New Testament Commentary 2 Timothy, pg. 3

8   2 Timothy 3:16-17

9   2 Timothy 1:4

10   Mark Kantrowitz." How Much Do You Need to Save for College?" savingforcollege.com. December 21, 2023

11   1 Timothy 5:23

12   Charles Spurgeon, *2 Thessalonians, 2 Timothy & Titus*, pg. 98

13   2 Timothy 4:11, 16

14   Matthew 28:19

15   Anazōpyreō, Strong's Greek Lexicon, Entry G329.

16   2 Timothy 1:8, 2 Timothy 2:1, 2 Timothy 3:14, 2 Timothy 4:2, respectively.

17   John MacArthur, *The MacArthur Study Bible*, 2nd Edition, 1 Timothy 1:18, pg. 1608.

18   James 1:17

19   John 16:7-8

20   Matthew 1:20

21   Matthew 3:16

22   Mark 1:12

23   2 Peter 1:3

24   Foxe: *Voices of the Martyrs*, pg. 465

25   Foxe: *Voices of the Martyrs*, pg. 468

26   Acts 9:16

27   2 Corinthians 11:23-28

28   Elisabeth Elliot, *Suffering Is Never for Nothing*. pg. 9

29   Matthew 16:24

30   Mark 8:38

31   John 3:16, Ephesians 2:8-9

32   Matthew 13:46

33 Acts 9:5-6

34 Acts 9:7

35 Acts 9:11-12

36 Acts 9:27-28

37 John MacArthur, *The MacArthur New Testament Commentary 2 Timothy*, pg. 27.

38 Hypotyposis, *Strong's Greek Lexicon*. Entry 5296

39 One Degree Off Course – Policies and Course Correction, https://www.lexipol.com/ Accessed March 1, 2024.

40 R. Larry Moyer, *101 Tips for Evangelism; Practical Ways to Enhance Your Witness*, pg. 20

41 2 Timothy 1:13 b. New English Translation. NET Bible® copyright ©1996-2017 by Biblical Studies Press.

42 Endyō, Strong's Lexicon, G1746,https://www.blueletterbible. org/ Accessed March 5th, 2024.

43 John 3:16

44 Romans 8:27

45 phylassō, Strong's Lexicon G5442 blueletterbible.org Accessed March 6, 2024

46 Charles Spurgeon, *2 Thessalonians, 2 Timothy & Titus Commentary*, pg. 129.

47 Mark 14:50, Matthew 26:73-75

48 John 21:15-17

49 Colossians 4:6

50 kolakeia, Strong's Greek Lexicon, G2850. blueletterbible.org Accessed March 21, 2024.

51 eulogia, Strong's Greek Lexicon, G2129. blueletterbible.org Accessed March 21, 2024.

52 Romans 16:1-2

53 Romans 16:3-4

54 2 Timothy 4:19

55 1 Corinthians 10:31

56 endynamoō Strong's Greek Lexicon, entry 1743. www. blueletterbible.org Accessed March 23, 2024

57 Hebrews 13:23

58 Endyō, Strong's Greek Lexicon. Entry 1746.

59 Proverbs 22:6

60 ḥānak, Strongs Hebrew Lexicon. Entry 2596.

61 2 Timothy 2:1

62 Acts 4:12

63 1 Corinthians 1:18

64 L'oreal Thompson Payton, "Americans check their phones 144

times a day. Here's how to cut back" fortune.com Accessed April 6, 2024.

65 Acts 18:5, Romans 16:21
66 Philippians 1:1, Colossians 1:1, 1 Thessalonians 1:1, 2 Thessalonians 1:1, Philemon 1:1
67 Judges 2:16-18.
68 1 Samuel 8:7
69 Isaiah 59:2 Jeremiah 11
70 Hosea 2, 14, Micah 7:18
71 Philippians 2:10-11
72 "Billy Graham: What's the Cost of Following Jesus Christ?" Billy Graham Evangelistic Association, August 2, 2017
73 Charles Spurgeon, Spurgeon Commentary 2 Thessalonians, 2 Timothy & Titus, pg. 140
74 *Kopiaō,* Strong's Greek Lexicon, Entry G2872
75 John MacArthur. *The MacArthur New Testament Commentary 2 Timothy.* Pg. 48.
76 Bio, alysiamontano.net, Accessed December 5, 2024
77 Revelation 1:18
78 2 Timothy 4:6
79 Jim Elliot quote.
80 John 6:37, Hebrews 10:14-18
81 Gideon Alper, "Most Frivolous Law Suits Filed." Aplerlaw.com
82 Revelation 13:8
83 Janet F. Williams, "No safe amount: Contrary to recent reports, drinking alcohol while pregnant is dangerous" American Academy of Pediatrics. Published March, 2011.
84 Matthew 7:21-23
85 John MacArthur, The MacArthur New Testament Commentary 2 Timothy, pg. 93.
86 2 Timothy 2:14
87 *Mōros,* Strong's Greek Lexicon. Entry 3474.
88 *Apaideutos,* Strong's Greek Lexicon. Entry 521.
89 Romans 12:2
90 John Adams, "Letter from John Adams to Massachusetts Militia," 11 October 1798.
91 Strong's Greek Concordance, Entry 1133.
92 Exodus 7:11-12, 22, Exodus 8:7.
93 Exodus 8:19
94 Charles Spurgeon, Spurgeon Commentary 2 Thessalonians, 2 Timothy, & Titus, pg. 211
95 Acts 13
96 Acts 14:20

Endnotes:

97 *Brephos,* Strong's Greek Lexicon, Entry 1025.

98 "The Benefits of Reading to Babies" Cleveland Clinic, October 27, 2020.

99 Information gleaned from an article by Mark Cartwright, "Johan Sebastian Bach" *World History Encyclopedia*. Published May 2023.

100 "Inspired" Merriam Webster Dictionary, Web. Accessed October 2024.

101 See Matthew 5:21-28, Matthew 12:3-5, Mark 2:25. Marl 6:6-8, Luke 11:31-32 and many others.

102 Matthew 19:28, Mark 4:11 and others.

103 John 8:11

104 Matthew 28:20

105 John MacArthur, The MacArthur New Testament Commentary, 2 Timothy, pg. 152

106 2 Kings 17:34, 2 Chronicles 12:1-2

107 Psalm 119:72

108 Psalm 119:77

109 Psalm 119:98

110 Psalm 119:105

111 Matthew 13:8

112 *Artios,* Strong's Greek Lexicon, G739.

113 Acts 20:19

114 Acts 20:20

115 Michael Brown, "3 Things You Should Know about 1 & 2 Timothy" www.ligonier.org, Accessed 11/23/2024.

116 John 5:22

117 Matthew 25:31-46

118 Revelation 20:11-15

119 2 Corinthians 5:10

120 Philippians 3:2

121 2 Timothy 3:14a

122 John MacArthur, *The MacArthur New Testament Commentary 2 Timothy*, pg. 189.

123 Philippians 1:21

124 Revelation 21:4

125 1 Corinthians 12:14-26

126 John MacArthur, The MacArthur New Testament Commentary 2 Timothy, pg. 204-205

127 John MacArthur, The MacArthur New Testament Commentary 2 Timothy, pg. 207

128 Acts 25:11

224

129 Charles Spurgeon. Spurgeon Commentary, *2 Thessalonians, 2 Timothy & Titus.* Pg. 253-254

130 Matthew 10:19b

131 Matthew 28:20

132 Tedd Tripp. *Shepherding a Child's Heart*, pg. 22

ACKNOWLEDGMENTS

First, a note of gratitude to my Lord and Savior, Jesus Christ, for His work transforming my life, saving me from my sin, and allowing me to play a part in building His kingdom through sharing His Word. To my husband, Jonathan Hager, for his unending support and encouragement with this project. A special thank you to my wonderful mother, Carol Arch, for crafting the study guide questions for this book. Thank you to Dr. R. Larry Moyer for your help and writing mentorship. Thank you to Ms. Kimberly Schumate and Ms. Becky Bayne for their editing and formatting expertise. A special thank you to my launch team for their hours of hard work.

ABOUT THE AUTHOR

Katherine Hager is passionate about supporting and encouraging women, but especially moms. Her writing ministry connects women to the Word of God as they walk through the seasons of motherhood. When she is not writing, Katherine enjoys spending time with her husband and their four children, and helps run their ministry for at-risk kids in central Texas. She loves open skies, vibrant sunsets, and spring weather perfect for outdoor play (minus the occasional rattlesnake).

Visit Katherine's website at https://equippedmama.com/ and sign up for her newsletter as she continues to write, speak, and present the Word to young moms.

Other Books by Katherine Hager

www.ingramcontent.com/pod-product-compliance
Lightning Source LLC
Chambersburg PA
CBHW021232130626
46554CB00004B/1449